easy to make!
Kids' Cakes
& Party Food

Good Housekeeping

easy to make!
Kids' Cakes
& Party Food

COLLINS & BROWN

First published in Great Britain in 2009
by Collins & Brown
10 Southcombe Street
London W14 0RA

An imprint of Anova Books Company Ltd

The Good Housekeeping website is
www.allaboutyou.com/goodhousekeeping

10 9 8 7 6 5 4 3 2 1

ISBN 978-1-84340-500-9

A catalogue record for this book is available from the British
Library.

Reproduction by Dot Gradations Ltd
Printed and bound by Times Offset, Malaysia

This book can be ordered direct from the publisher. Contact the
marketing department, but try your bookshop first.

www.anovabooks.com

NOTES

- Both metric and imperial measures are given for the recipes. Follow either set of measures, not a mixture of both, as they are not interchangeable.
- All spoon measures are level.
  1 tsp = 5ml spoon; 1 tbsp = 15ml spoon.
- Ovens and grills must be preheated to the specified temperature.
- Use sea salt and freshly ground black pepper unless otherwise suggested.
- Fresh herbs should be used unless dried herbs are specified in a recipe.
- Medium eggs should be used except where otherwise specified. Free-range eggs are recommended.
- Note that certain recipes, including mayonnaise, lemon curd and some icings and frostings, contain raw or lightly cooked eggs. The young, elderly, pregnant women and anyone with an immune-deficiency disease should avoid these, because of the slight risk of salmonella.
- Calorie, fat and carbohydrate counts per serving are provided for the recipes.
- If you are following a gluten- or dairy-free diet, check the labels on all pre-packaged food goods.
- Recipe serving suggestions do not take gluten- or dairy-free diets into account.

Picture credits
Photographers: Nicki Dowey pages 10, 18, 20, 21, 23, 26, 28, 33, 34, 35, 36, 38, 39, 40, 43, 45, 46, 51, 52, 54, 55, 56, 59, 60, 61, 63, 64, 69, 70, 71, 72, 73, 74, 75, 76, 78, 79, 80, 82, 83, 85, 86, 87, 88, 89, 91, 94, 95, 96, 97, 99, 101, 102, 103, 104, 105, 106, 107, 108, 109, 110, 111, 112, 113, 114, 115, 118, 119, 120, 121, 122, 123, 124, 125, 126; Craig Robertson (Basics photography plus page 41); Lucinda Symons (page 100).

Contents

Foreword

Children's birthday parties are magical occasions. The cake, the party food, the games and presents, they all add to the fun atmosphere. It should be a pleasurable event for you too; a time to remember fondly. What it shouldn't be is stressful and difficult. That's why we've put together Kids' Cakes and Party Food. It's packed with gorgeous birthday cakes and appetising party food and drinks, as well as tips for making the day run more smoothly.

The cake is the highlight of any birthday party and we've created a selection that caters for all abilities. Whether you're a dab hand at handling icing or you're a complete novice who trembles at the thought of getting a piping bag in your hand, you can create a wondrous cake that will elicit oohs and aahs from the party guests.

The book includes over 100 recipes for party success. All the recipes have been triple tested in the Good Housekeeping kitchens to make sure they work every time.

Emma

Emma Marsden
Cookery Editor
Good Housekeeping

The Basics

Kids' parties

It's the day that children look forward to all year – their birthday. Don't get stressed; if you're organised and don't try to take on too much, then it will be a day your child – and you – will always remember. It's meant to be fun, so don't worry too much if they eat only the sweet treats – they'll be back to their healthier diet tomorrow!

Holding a party

The venue

There's no need to hold the party at your house if you're worried about mess. Check out your local church, community or village hall: they often hire out the space for private parties and there's usually a simple kitchen on the premises where you can store food in the fridges. You'll also be able to make tea and coffee for the parents if they're staying to watch over younger children.

- Some venues offer a party service, providing bouncy castles, games, bubble machines and music, depending on your budget.
- Make the most of good weather if it's a summer birthday and hold a picnic party in your local park – check bylaws first with your local council.
- Share party costs with other parents if birthdays fall close together.

Invitations

It's easy to tailor invitations to your theme with some coloured card and pens:

- Hearts cut out from pink card
- Spiders' webs drawn with silver pen on to a hexagonal piece of black card
- Celebrity party – make VIP backstage passes
- Witches' hats made from black card

Quantities

Remember not to overcater: your guests will be excited and won't eat or drink as much as you might expect. For each guest, allow:

- 3 small sandwiches and 2 savoury bites
- 2 sweet treats
- 1 slice of birthday cake
- 1–2 glasses of smoothie, punch or lemonade. Any extra-thirsty children can drink water or weak squash. If you're holding a sports party, take along large bottles of water or diluted squash

Don't attempt to make everything from scratch – you want to enjoy the party too. Choose a few recipes to cook and add to them with cherry tomatoes, carrot sticks, dips, crisps and ice cream.

Decorations and activities

- Decorate the venue with balloons, or tie them to chairs, then give one to each guest when they leave.
- Look in the bin ends in DIY shops for rolls of wallpaper; you can roll them out on the table, white side up, to use as a tablecloth and drawing pad.
- Put packs of cheap coloured pencils on the table so that the children can have fun drawing on wallpaper or placemats.
- Make your own piñata: blow up a balloon, knot and tie on string. Cover it with papier mâché and hang up to dry. When dry, burst the balloon and cut a small hole at the top adjacent to the string. Fill with sweets, confetti and plastic toys and seal the hole with strips of paper. Paint with fun designs and leave to dry. On the day of the party, hang up in a safe place (away from lightbulbs) with plenty of space. Get the children to take turns in using a sawn-off broom handle to hit the piñata until it bursts.
- If you are relaxed about mess, set up a table with bowls of coloured icing and edible decorations. Let the children decorate fairy cakes and biscuits.
- Arrange crisps or sweets in small colourful plastic buckets or bowls.
- Fit traditional party games around the party theme, such as musical chairs or wizards and witches apple bobbing.

Party themes

Themes help you to build the celebration around one idea. Make it as simple as a colour, a favourite cartoon character or pirates and princesses. Choosing just three or four themed ideas for the food and table decorations will stop your stress levels rising and ensure that the kids have a fabulous time. Fill in the gaps with easy-to-make sandwiches, dips and sweet treats. Here are a few ideas to get you started...

Princess pink party

- Ask the guests to dress in pink and white
- Use pink paper as a tablecloth and scatter with silver heart and star decorations
- Arrange pink cup cakes in a large heart shape on a board or platter
- Menu suggestions: heart-shaped sandwiches (see page 26), Chocolate Butterfly Cakes (see page 103), Pastel Meringues (see page 34), Sleeping Beauty's Castle (see page 53), Berry Smoothie (see page 120), Fairy Cocktail (see page 124).

Witches and wizards party

- Lay the table with orange, black or green paper or wallpaper
- Scatter the table with plastic mice, bats, spiders and snakes
- Make a cauldron to hold punch or sweets by covering a bowl with black paper and silver stars
- Decorate fairy cakes with orange icing and draw on spiders' webs
- Menu suggestions: Cheese Wands (see page 84), Mini Savoury Tarts (see page 00), Creepy-crawly Cake (see page 50), Meringue Bones (see page 102), Mud and Worm Juice (see page 119), Witches' Brew (see page 118).

Jungle party

- Look out for themed paper plates and cups
- Get an artistic friend to be in charge of animal face painting
- Organise a jungle treasure hunt in the garden or outside space at the venue, with sweets and plastic animals as prizes
- Menu suggestions: Sticky Chicken Drumsticks (see page 73), Tiger Cake (see page 65), Dinosaur Biscuits (see page 97), Mango Banana Smoothie (see page 125), Jungle Juice (see page 121).

Party cakes: getting started

You don't need specialist equipment for making party cakes; in fact, you probably have many of these items in your kitchen already.

Weighing and measuring

Scales

Accurate measurement is essential when baking. The most accurate scale is the electronic type, capable of weighing up to 2kg (4½lb) or 5kg (11lb) in increments of 1–5g. Buy one with a flat platform on which you can put your own bowl or measuring jug, and always remember to set the scale to zero before adding the ingredients.

Measuring jugs

These can be plastic or glass, and are available in sizes ranging from 500ml (18fl oz) to 2 litres (3½ pints), or even 3 litres (5¼ pints). Have two – a large one and a small one – marked with both metric and imperial measurements.

Measuring cups

Commonly used in the US, these are used for measuring liquid and dry ingredients. Cups are bought in sets of ¼, ⅓, ½ and 1 cups. A standard 1 cup measure is equivalent to about 250ml (9fl oz).

Measuring spoons

Useful for the smallest units, accurate spoon measurements go from 1.25ml (¼ tsp) to 15ml (1 tbsp).

Mixing

Bowls

For mixing large quantities, such as cake mixtures, you will need at least two large bowls, including one with a diameter of up to 38cm (15in).
- Plastic or glass bowls are best if you need to use them in the microwave.
- Steel bowls with a rubber foot will keep their grip on the worksurface.
- Bowls with gently tapered sides – much wider at the rim than at the base – are useful for mixing dough.

Spoons

For general mixing, the cheap and sturdy wooden spoon still can't be beaten, but equivalents made from thermoplastic materials are heatproof and may suit you better. A large metal spoon for folding ingredients together is also invaluable when baking.

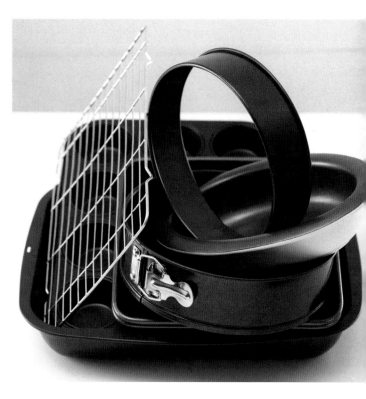

Bakeware

As well as being thin enough to conduct heat quickly and efficiently, bakeware should be sturdy enough not to warp when heated. Most bakeware is made from aluminium, and it may have enamel or non-stick coatings.

Cake tins Available in many shapes and sizes, tins may be single-piece, loose-based or springform.
Loaf tins Available in various sizes, one of the most useful is a 900g (2lb) tin.
Pie tins and muffin tins You should have both single-piece tins and loose-based tins for flans and pies.
Oven-safe silicone is safe to touch straight from the oven, is inherently non-stick and is also flexible – making it easy to remove muffins and other bakes.

Other useful utensils

Baking sheets (two)	Cooling racks (two)
Spatulas	Palette knife
Wire whisks	Ruler
Fine sieve	Dredger
Microplane grater	Serrated knife
Rolling pin	Icing bag and piping
Thin skewers	nozzles
Cookie cutters	Vegetable peeler

Electrical equipment

Food processor For certain tasks, such as making breadcrumbs or pastry or for chopping large quantities of nuts, food processors are unbeatable. Most come with a number of attachments – dough hooks, graters, slicers – which are worth having, even if only for occasional use.
Blender These are less versatile than food processors, but unmatched for certain tasks, such as puréeing fruit. The traditional jug blender is great but some cooks prefer a hand-held stick blender, which can be used directly in a pan, bowl or jug.
Freestanding mixer An electric mixer may be a good investment if you do a lot of baking, but decide first whether you have space in your kitchen. They are big and heavy to store.
Electric hand mixer Useful for creaming together butter and sugar in baking and for making meringues. They don't take up a lot of space and can be packed away easily.

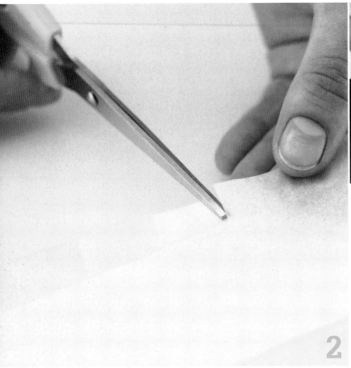

Lining tins

When making cakes, you usually need to grease and/or line the tin with greaseproof paper before filling it with cake mixture. Lightly grease the tin first to help keep the paper in place. You will need to use different techniques according to the shape of the tin.

Round tin

1 Put the tin on a sheet of greaseproof paper and draw a circle around its circumference. Cut out the circle just inside the drawn line.

2 Cut a strip or strips about 2cm (³/₄ in) wider than the depth of the tin and fold up one long edge of each strip by 1cm (¹/₂in). Make cuts, about 2.5cm (1in) apart, through the folded edge of the strip(s) up to the fold line.

3 Lightly grease the tin with butter, making sure it is completely coated.

4 Press the strip(s) on to the sides of the tin so that the snipped edge sits on the base.

5 Lay the circle in the bottom of the tin and grease the paper.

Swiss roll tin

Use this method for Swiss roll or other shallow baking tins.

1 Lightly grease the tin with butter, making sure it is completely coated.

2 Cut a piece of baking parchment into a rectangle 7.5cm (3in) wider and longer than the tin. Press it into the tin and cut at the corners, then fold to fit neatly. Grease all over.

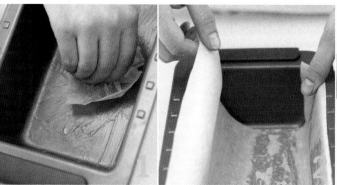

Loaf tin

1 Lightly grease the tin with butter, making sure it is completely coated.

2 Cut out a sheet of greaseproof paper to the same length as the base and wide enough to cover both the base and the long sides. Press it into position, making sure that it sits snugly in the corners.

3 Now cut another sheet to the same width as the base and long enough to cover both the base and the ends of the tin. Press into place. Grease the paper all over.

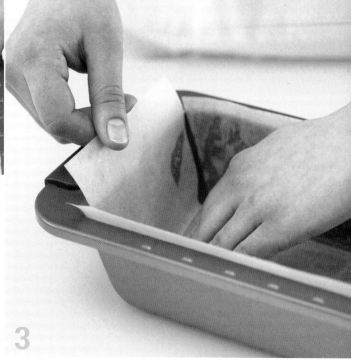

Perfect lining

Use greaseproof paper for all cakes and baking parchment for roulades and meringues.
Apply the butter with a small piece of greaseproof paper.
Don't grease too thickly – this 'fries' the edges of the cake.

Square tin

1 Cut out a square of greaseproof paper slightly smaller than the base of the tin. Cut four strips about 2cm (³/₄in) wider than the depth of the tin and fold up one of the longest edges of each strip by 1cm (¹/₂in).

2 Lightly grease the tin with butter, making sure it is coated on all sides and in the corners.

3 Cut one strip to the length of the side of the tin and press into place in one corner then along the length of the strip, with the narrow folded section sitting on the base. Continue, cutting to fit into the corners, to cover all four sides.

4 Lay the square on the base of the tin, then grease the paper, taking care not to move the side strips.

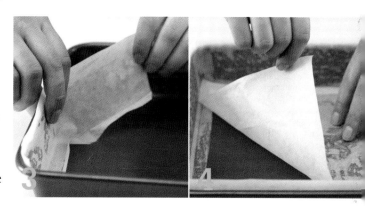

Making cakes

Many of the party cakes in this book are based on a Victoria sponge, which can be made by creaming the mixture or using the all-in-one method.

Creaming

A classic creamed (Victoria) sponge can be used to make many cakes, including chocolate or fruit. Use the chart opposite to check the quantities you will need.

1 Preheat the oven to 180°C (160°C fan oven) mark 4. Grease and line a cake tin following the instructions on pages 14–15. Put the butter and sugar in a bowl and beat with an electric whisk or wooden spoon until pale, soft and creamy.

2 Beat the eggs and gradually add to the butter and sugar mixture, beating well until the mixture is thick and of dropping consistency. If you like, add a spoonful of the flour while adding the eggs to prevent curdling.

3 Gently fold in the flour using a large metal spoon or spatula, then spoon the mixture into the prepared tin(s), level the surface and bake.

Short-cut cake

Lay one or two family-sized loaf cakes (available from supermarkets) next to each other on a cake board, depending on the size of finished cake required. Cover with a thin layer of bought vanilla or chocolate buttercream-style icing, then cover with ready-to-roll icing and decorate with edible decorations or plastic figurines. Alternatively, cover with a thicker layer of buttercream if you like and omit the ready-to-roll icing.

Variations

Chocolate Replace 3 tbsp flour with cocoa powder. Sandwich the cakes together with vanilla or chocolate buttercream.
Citrus Add the finely grated zest of 1 orange, lemon or lime to the mixture. Sandwich the cakes together with orange, lemon or lime buttercream.

All-in-one

1 Preheat the oven to 180°C (160°C fan oven) mark 4. Grease and line a cake tin following the instructions on pages 14–15. Put the butter, sugar, eggs, flour and baking powder in a large bowl or mixer.

2 Using an electric whisk, mix slowly to start, then increase the speed slightly until well combined. Fold in any remaining ingredients, such as fruit, then spoon into the prepared tin(s) and bake.

Cooling cakes

Sponge cakes should be taken out of their tins soon after baking. Invert on to a wire rack covered with sugar-dusted baking parchment.

Testing sponges

1 Gently press the centre of the sponge. It should feel springy. If you have to put it back into the oven, close the door gently so that the vibrations don't cause the cake to sink in the centre.

Victoria sponge chart

CAKE TIN SIZE	15cm (6in) round 12.5cm (5in) square	18cm (7in) round 15cm (6in) square	20.5cm (8in) round 18cm (7in) square
Butter, softened	125g (4oz)	175g (6oz)	225g (8oz)
Caster sugar	125g (4oz)	175g (6oz)	225g (8oz)
Medium eggs	2	3	4
Self-raising flour	125g (4oz)	175g (6oz)	225g (8oz)
Baking powder	1 tsp	1½ tsp	2 tsp
Baking time	20 minutes	25 minutes	25–30 minutes

Note: For larger cakes (from 23cm/9in upwards), it is advisable to use the Madeira cake recipe on page 18.

2 Sift the flours into a mixing bowl, add the butter, sugar, eggs and lemon juice or milk. Mix together with a wooden spoon, then beat for 1–2 minutes until smooth and glossy. Alternatively, use an electric mixer and beat for 1 minute only. Add any flavourings if required and mix until well blended.

3 Turn the mixture into the prepared tin and spread evenly. Give the tin a sharp tap to remove any air pockets. Make a depression in the centre of the mixture to ensure a level surface.

Madeira cake (quick mix method)

1 Preheat the oven to 170°C (150°C fan oven) mark 3. Grease and line a deep cake tin following the instructions on pages 14–15. Use the chart below to check the quantities you will need.

4 Bake in the centre of the oven following the baking times in the chart belows as a guide, or until the cake springs back when lightly pressed in the centre.

5 Leave the cake to cool in the tin, then remove and cool completely on a wire rack. Wrap in clingfilm or foil and store in a cool place until required.

Madeira cake chart

CAKE TIN SIZE	20.5cm (8in) square 23cm (9in) round	23cm (9in) square 25.5cm (10in) round	25.5cm (10in) square 28cm (11in) round
Plain flour	225g (8oz)	250g (9oz)	275g (10oz)
Self-raising flour	225g (8oz)	250g (9oz)	275g (10oz)
Unsalted butter, softened	400g (14oz)	450g (1lb)	500g (1lb 2oz)
Caster sugar	400g (14oz)	450g (1lb)	500g (1lb 2oz)
Medium eggs	7	8	10
Lemon juice or milk	3½ tbsp	4 tbsp	4½ tbsp
Baking time (approx.)	1¾–2 hours	1¾–2 hours	2–2¼ hours

Splitting and filling a cake

Sponge cakes are often made in two tins, but can also be made in a deeper tin, then split and filled with jam, buttercream, cream or mascarpone with sliced fruit.

1 Allow the cake to cool completely before splitting.

2 Use a knife with a shallow thin blade, such as a ham knife, a bread knife or a carving knife. Cut a notch from top to bottom on one side so you will know where to line the pieces up after you've filled the cake. Cut midway between top and bottom, about 30 per cent of the way through the cake. Turn the cake while cutting, taking care to keep the blade parallel with the base, until you have cut all the way around.

3 Continue cutting until you have cut all the way through, then carefully lift off the top of the cake.

4 Warm jam slightly to make it easier to spread, or make sure buttercream is not too firm, then spread over the base, stopping 1cm (1/2in) from the edge.

5 Carefully put the top layer of cake on top of the filling and gently pat into place.

Apricot Glaze

Brush cakes with apricot glaze before covering with marzipan or with ready-to-roll icing (sugar paste). It can also be used to glaze fruit finishes on cakes and tarts. You will only need 3–4 tbsp at a time, but apricot glaze keeps well in the refrigerator, so it is worth making a larger quantity. Warm very gently before using.

To make 450g (1lb), you will need:
450g (1lb) apricot jam, 2 tbsp water.

1 Put the jam and water into a saucepan and heat gently, stirring occasionally, until melted.

2 Boil the jam rapidly for 1 minute, then strain through a sieve. Using a wooden spoon, rub through as much fruit as possible. Discard the skins left in the sieve.

3 Pour the glaze into a clean, hot jar, then seal with a clean lid and cool. Store in the refrigerator for up to two months.

Covering cakes

There are lots of options for covering cakes, depending on the finish you require. Marzipan gives an even, flat surface for covering with sugar paste or royal icing, particularly on fruit cakes. But if you want to avoid marzipan because of nut allergies, a Victoria sponge or Madeira cake can simply be covered with buttercream or apricot glaze, followed by a layer of ready-to-roll icing (sugar paste).

Cook's Tip

Ready-made icings, cake boards and a wide range of decorations are available from supermarkets and specialist cake decorating shops or via the internet.

Covering a cake with marzipan

Once you have applied the marzipan, you will need to allow time for it to dry before covering with icing. Home-made marzipan takes a little longer to dry out than the ready-made variety.

1 Trim the top of the cake level if necessary, then turn the cake over to give you a flat surface to work on. Place on the cake board, which should be at least 5cm (2in) larger than the cake. Brush the cake with apricot glaze (see page 19).

2 Dust the worksurface with sifted icing sugar, then roll out half the marzipan to fit the top of the cake. Lift the marzipan on top of the cake and smooth over, neatening the edges.

3 Cut a piece of string the same height as the cake with the marzipan topping, and another to fit around the diameter of the cake. Roll out the remaining marzipan and, using the string as a guide, trim the marzipan to size. Roll up the marzipan strip loosely. Place one end against the side of the cake and unroll the marzipan around the cake to cover it. Use a palette knife to smooth over the sides and joins of the marzipan.

4 Leave the cake in a cool, dry place to dry out thoroughly for at least 24 hours before covering with ready-to-roll icing. Allow to dry for at least two days before applying royal icing.

Covering a cake with ready-to-roll icing (sugar paste)

Ready-to-roll icing is pliable and can be used to cover cakes or moulded into decorative shapes. You can make your own (see below), but blocks of ready-to-roll icing (sugar paste) are available in a variety of colours from supermarkets and specialist cake decorating shops. A 450g (1lb) pack will cover an 18cm (7in) cake. Wrap any unused icing in clingfilm to stop it drying out and store in a cool, dry place.

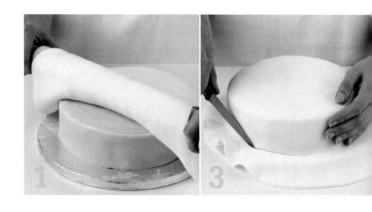

1 Dust the worksurface and rolling pin with sifted icing sugar. Knead the icing until pliable, then roll out into a round or square 5–7.5cm (2–3in) larger than the cake all round. Lift the icing on top of the cake and allow it to drape over the edges.

2 Dust your hands with sifted icing sugar and press the icing on to the sides of the cake, easing it down to the board.

3 Using a sharp knife, trim off the excess icing at the base to neaten. Reserve the trimmings to make decorations if required.

4 Using your fingers dusted with a little sifted icing sugar, gently rub the surface in a circular movement to buff the icing and make it smooth.

Home-made Sugar Paste

To make about 450g (1lb), enough to cover the top and sides of an 18cm (7in) round cake, you will need:
1 medium egg white, 1 tbsp liquid glucose, 500g (1lb 2oz) icing sugar, sifted, plus extra to dust.

1 Put the egg white and liquid glucose into a clean bowl, blending with a wooden spoon to break up the egg white. Add the icing sugar and mix until the icing begins to bind together. Knead with your fingers until the mixture forms a rough ball. Put the sugar paste on a surface lightly dusted with sifted icing sugar and knead thoroughly until smooth, pliable and free from cracks.

2 If the sugar paste is too soft to handle and is rather sticky, knead in some more sifted icing sugar until firm and pliable. If the sugar paste is dry and too firm, knead in a little boiled water until the paste becomes soft and pliable.

3 Wrap the sugar paste completely in clingfilm or store in a polythene bag with all the air excluded.

Covering a cake with royal icing or buttercream

Buttercream can be spread directly on to the cake; if you are using royal icing, first cover the cake with apricot glaze (see page 19).

1 Stir royal icing or buttercream just before using, to make sure it is easy to spread.

2 Put the cake on a plate or cake board and use a palette knife to spread the icing evenly over the cake.

Icings

Buttercream

To cover the top of a 20.5cm (8in) cake, you will need:
75g (3oz) unsalted butter, 175g (6oz) icing sugar, sifted, a few drops of vanilla extract, 1–2 tbsp milk.

1 Soften the butter in a mixing bowl, then beat until light and fluffy.

2 Gradually stir in the remaining ingredients and beat until smooth.

Variations

Citrus Replace the vanilla with a little grated orange, lemon or lime zest, and use some of the fruit's juice in place of the milk.
Chocolate Blend 1 tbsp cocoa powder with 2 tbsp boiling water. Cool, then add to the mixture in place of the milk.
Coloured For a strong colour, use food colouring paste; liquid colouring gives a paler effect (see Cook's Tip).

Royal

Royal icing can be bought in packs from supermarkets. Simply add water or egg white to use.

To make 450g (1lb), enough to cover the top and sides of a 20cm (8in) cake, you will need:
2 medium egg whites, 1/4 tsp lemon juice, 450g (1lb) icing sugar, sifted, 1 tsp glycerine.

1 Put the egg whites and lemon juice into a clean bowl. Stir to break up the egg whites.

2 Add sufficient icing sugar to mix to the consistency of unwhipped cream. Continue mixing and adding small quantities of icing sugar every few minutes until the desired consistency is reached, mixing well and gently beating after each addition of icing sugar. The icing should be smooth, glossy and light, almost like a cold meringue in texture, but not aerated. Do not add the icing sugar too quickly or it will produce a dull heavy icing. Stir in the glycerine until well blended.

3 Alternatively, for large quantities of royal icing, use a food mixer on the lowest speed, following the same instructions as before.

4 Allow the icing to settle before using it; cover the surface with a piece of damp clingfilm and seal well, excluding all the air.

5 Stir the icing thoroughly before use to disperse any air bubbles, then adjust the consistency if necessary by adding more sifted icing sugar.

Glacé

To make 225g (8oz), enough to cover 18 fairy cakes, you will need:
225g (8oz) icing sugar, few drops of vanilla or almond flavouring (optional), 2–3 tbsp boiling water, food colouring (optional).

1 Sift the icing sugar into a bowl. Add a few drops of flavouring, if you like.

2 Using a wooden spoon, gradually stir in enough water until the mixture is the consistency of thick cream. Beat until white and smooth and the icing is thick enough to coat the back of the spoon. Add colouring, if you like, and use at once.

Variations

Orange or lemon Replace the water with strained orange or lemon juice.
Chocolate Sift 2 tsp cocoa powder with the icing sugar.
Coloured Add a few drops of liquid food colouring, or use food colouring paste for a stronger colour.

Cook's Tip

Food colourings are available in liquid, paste or powder form. Add minute amounts with the tip of a cocktail stick until the desired colour is achieved.

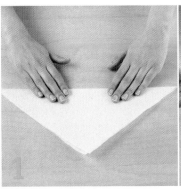  

Piping bags

Piping bags can be bought from specialist cake decorating shops, or you can make your own from greaseproof paper. A bag with a very small hole will allow you to make delicate patterns or writing; larger holes are more suitable for textured effects on the cake surface.

1 Cut a piece of greaseproof paper about 20.5cm (8in) square. Fold in half diagonally.

2 Bring the two corners of the long side of the triangle up to meet the top of the triangle, one in front of it and one behind, to make a cone.

3 Holding all three corners of the triangle together firmly, make sure the tip of the cone is closed, then fold over the corners and pinch all around the top of the cone to secure. Snip off the tip. Test the thickness of the line on a piece of non-stick baking parchment.

Cook's Tip

Writing icing pens are available in different sizes. Some are fine enough for finer writing while others are more suitable for piping designs.

Frostings

Seven-minute

To make about 175g (6oz), enough to cover the top and sides of an 18cm (7in) cake, you will need:
1 medium egg white, 175g (6oz) caster sugar, 2 tbsp water, pinch of salt, pinch of cream of tartar.

1 Put all the ingredients into a heatproof bowl and whisk lightly using an electric hand whisk.

2 Put the bowl over a pan of hot water and heat, whisking continuously, until the mixture thickens sufficiently to stand in peaks. This will take about 7 minutes.

3 Pour the frosting over the top of the cake and spread with a palette knife.

Vanilla

To make about 175g (6oz), enough to cover the top and sides of an 18cm (7in) cake, you will need:
150g (5oz) icing sugar, sifted, 5 tsp vegetable oil, 1 tbsp milk, few drops of vanilla extract.

1 Put the icing sugar in a bowl and, using a wooden spoon, beat in the oil, milk and vanilla extract until smooth.

Making biscuits and cookies

Home-made biscuits are always welcome; the only drawback is they are so moreish – you'll need all your willpower to stay away from the biscuit tin.

Cookie troubleshooting

Although very simple in their composition, biscuits can be surprisingly prone to baking problems because they cook so quickly. It's as well to be aware of the possible problems and to know what can cause them. Following a few key points should minimise the potential pitfalls.

Use a shiny-based baking sheet: a darker-coloured sheet will absorb a greater amount of heat and may burn the undersides of the biscuits.

Don't overcrowd the biscuits on the baking sheet or in the oven – air needs to circulate all around them. If you are baking more than one sheet at a time, make sure they are on oven shelves at least 20.5cm (8in) apart.

Turn the baking sheet(s) around once or twice during baking. Most ovens get hotter in some places than in others, and this can cause uneven cooking.

If you are cooking more than one sheet, be prepared to have them bake at different speeds. Watch them closely for uneven cooking.

Start testing biscuits slightly before you expect them to be cooked. And watch them very closely during the final minutes, as they can go from perfect to overcooked in a matter of only a few seconds.

Like cakes, biscuits must be transferred to a wire rack while they are still hot. The hot baking sheet will continue to cook them, and steam will build up underneath, which can make the bases soggy. As soon as they are cooked, lift the biscuits from the baking sheet and transfer to a wire rack to cool. Some biscuits, however (particularly those made with syrup), need to be left on the baking sheet to firm up a little before they are transferred to a rack.

Ideally, cool the biscuits on a fairly fine-meshed rack.

If possible, raise the rack by putting it on supports so that it is at least a few centimetres higher than the worksurface underneath: the more air circulating underneath, the crisper the bases will be.

If the biscuits are tough or dry, the dough may have been overworked or too much flour may have been added.

Biscuits that spread too much during baking contain too much butter or sugar, or the mixture may have been overbeaten.

A cake-like texture indicates that too much flour was used or the biscuits were baked at too high a temperature.

Rolled Vanilla Biscuits

The easiest way to make biscuits of consistent thickness is by rolling and then cutting using a biscuit cutter. The dough must be firm enough to roll to a thickness of 3mm (⅛in).

You will need:

175g (6oz) unsalted butter, softened, 200g (7oz) golden caster sugar, 350g (12oz) plain flour, 1 medium egg, 2 tsp vanilla bean paste, 2 tbsp golden icing sugar.

1 Preheat the oven to 200°C (180°C fan oven) mark 6. Put the butter, caster sugar, flour, egg and vanilla bean paste into a food processor and whiz to combine. Alternatively, cream the butter and sugar, and then stir in the flour, egg and vanilla.

2 Put the dough on a large sheet of baking parchment. Press the dough gently but firmly with the palm of your hand to flatten it slightly, then put another sheet of baking parchment on top – this will prevent the dough from sticking.

3 Use a rolling pin to roll out the dough to 3mm (⅛in) thick, and then remove the top sheet of baking parchment.

4 Using 6.5cm (2½in) cutters, stamp out biscuits, leaving a 3mm (⅛in) gap between each one.

5 Peel off the trimmings around the shapes, then slide the baking parchment and biscuits on to a flat baking sheet.

6 Re-roll the trimmings between two new sheets of baking parchment, then stamp out shapes as before and slide on to another baking sheet.

7 Bake the biscuits for 10–12 minutes until pale golden. Cool for a few minutes, then transfer to a wire rack to cool completely.

8 Dust the biscuits with sifted icing sugar. Store in an airtight container for up to five days.

Sandwiches with a difference

Party sandwiches don't have to be dull. All you need is a little imagination and lots of delicious fillings...

Aim for variety

There are all sorts of interesting breads and rolls available that are perfect for perking up sandwiches.

- Children love miniature versions of grown-up food; hearty sandwiches may put them off tucking in.
- Look out for mini wholemeal pittas and dinner rolls.
- Flavoured wraps are a quick and easy way to make sandwiches for large numbers and cost-effective too – once filled and rolled they can be sliced into bite-sized pieces.
- Sliced bread can be transformed into fun shapes with cookie cutters – try heart or star-shaped sandwiches for the party princess, farmyard animals or dinosaurs and even cars. The possibilities are endless. Use the same shaped cutter to cut out slices of cheese or ham for a neat fit.
- Arrange alternate sandwich squares made with white and wholemeal bread to make a draughts board.
- To make Pinwheel Sandwiches, shown left, see page 88.

Getting ahead

- Chilling a loaf will make it easier to cut.
- Don't forget to soften the butter to make it easier to spread.
- Fillings can be made a day ahead, covered and stored in the refrigerator until ready to assemble the sandwiches.
- Rolls and sandwiches can be made up to 3 hours ahead. Cover with a slightly damp teatowel, then foil or clingfilm, and store in the refrigerator.
- Prepare a few plain buttered rolls for fussy eaters.

Four easy fillings

These fillings are nutritious and quick to prepare. Each recipe will make enough to fill 3 rounds of sliced bread sandwiches.

Egg Mayonnaise

Put 3 medium eggs in a small pan and cover with water. Bring to the boil and cook for 6 minutes. Drain and run them under cold water. Peel, then mash the eggs with 2 tbsp mayonnaise. Stir in mustard and cress.

Tuna and Sweetcorn

Mix together 1 x 185g tin tuna in spring water with 1 x 200g tin sweetcorn, drained, and 2 tbsp mayonnaise.

Chunky Hummus

Mix together 1 x 200g tub hummus with $\frac{1}{4}$ cucumber, chopped, and 4 medium tomatoes, seeded and chopped.

Two-cheese and Spring Onion

Grate 100g ($3\frac{1}{2}$oz) mild Cheddar and 100g ($3\frac{1}{2}$oz) red Leicester cheese into a bowl. Stir in 4 finely chopped spring onions and 1 tbsp mayonnaise.

Three basic dips

Arrange a variety of dips with a pile of tempting, colourful vegetables such as carrot, celery and cucumber sticks, slices of different coloured pepper and cherry tomatoes.

Cherry Tomato and Pesto

Roughly chop 6 cherry tomatoes and stir into a tub of fresh pesto with 2 tbsp natural yogurt.

Cucumber and Yogurt

Seed and chop $\frac{1}{4}$ cucumber and put into a bowl with 1 tbsp freshly chopped mint. Stir in 150g (5oz) Greek yogurt.

Herby Cheese

Beat together 300g (10oz) herbed cream cheese with 4 tbsp mayonnaise and 2 tbsp freshly chopped parsley.

Food storage and hygiene

Storing food properly and preparing it in a hygienic way is important to ensure that food remains as nutritious and flavourful as possible, and to reduce the risk of food poisoning.

Hygiene

When you are preparing food, always follow these important guidelines:

Wash your hands thoroughly before handling food and again between handling different types of food, such as raw and cooked meat and poultry. If you have any cuts or grazes on your hands, be sure to keep them covered with a waterproof plaster.

Wash down worksurfaces regularly with a mild detergent solution or multi-surface cleaner.

Use a dishwasher if available. Otherwise, wear rubber gloves for washing-up, so that the water temperature can be hotter than unprotected hands can bear. Change drying-up cloths and cleaning cloths regularly. Note that leaving dishes to drain is more hygienic than drying them with a teatowel.

Keep raw and cooked foods separate, especially meat, fish and poultry. Wash kitchen utensils in between preparing raw and cooked foods. Never put cooked or ready-to-eat foods directly on to a surface which has just had raw fish, meat or poultry on it.

Keep pets out of the kitchen if possible; or make sure they stay away from worksurfaces. Never allow animals on to worksurfaces.

Shopping

Always choose fresh ingredients in prime condition from stores and markets that have a regular turnover of stock to ensure you buy the freshest produce possible.

Make sure items are within their 'best before' or 'use by' date. (Foods with a longer shelf life have a 'best before' date; more perishable items have a 'use by' date.)

Pack frozen and chilled items in an insulated cool bag at the check-out and put them into the freezer or refrigerator as soon as you get home.

During warm weather in particular, buy perishable foods just before you return home. When packing items at the check-out, sort them according to where you will store them when you get home – the refrigerator, freezer, storecupboard, vegetable rack, fruit bowl, etc. This will make unpacking easier – and quicker.

The storecupboard

Although storecupboard ingredients will generally last a long time, correct storage is important:

Always check packaging for storage advice – even with familiar foods, because storage requirements may change if additives, sugar or salt have been reduced. Check storecupboard foods for their 'best before' or 'use by' date and do not use them if the date has passed.

Keep all food cupboards scrupulously clean and make sure food containers and packets are properly sealed.

Once opened, treat canned foods as though fresh. Always transfer the contents to a clean container, cover and keep in the refrigerator. Similarly, jars, sauce bottles and cartons should be kept chilled after opening. (Check the label for safe storage times after opening.)

Transfer dry goods such as sugar, flour, rice and pasta to airtight, moisture-proof containers. When supplies are used up, wash the container well and thoroughly dry before refilling with new supplies.

Store oils in a dark cupboard away from any heat source as heat and light can make them turn rancid and affect their colour. For the same reason, buy olive oil in dark green bottles.

Store vinegars in a cool place; they can turn bad in a warm environment.

Store dried herbs, spices and flavourings in a cool, dark cupboard or in dark jars. Buy in small quantities as their flavour will not last indefinitely.

Refrigerator storage

Fresh food needs to be kept in the cool temperature of the refrigerator to keep it in good condition and discourage the growth of harmful bacteria. Store day-to-day perishable items, such as opened jams and jellies, mayonnaise and bottled sauces, in the refrigerator along with eggs and dairy products, fruit juices, bacon, fresh and cooked meat (on separate shelves), and salads and vegetables (except potatoes, which don't suit being stored in the cold). A refrigerator should be kept at an operating temperature of 4–5°C.

It is worth investing in a refrigerator thermometer to ensure the correct temperature is maintained. To ensure your refrigerator is functioning effectively for safe food storage, follow these guidelines:

To avoid bacterial cross-contamination, store cooked and raw foods on separate shelves, putting cooked foods on the top shelf. Ensure that all items are well wrapped.

Never put hot food into the refrigerator, as this will cause the internal temperature of the refrigerator to rise.

Avoid overfilling the refrigerator, as this restricts the circulation of air and prevents the appliance from working properly.

It can take some time for the refrigerator to return to the correct operating temperature once the door has been opened, so don't leave it open any longer than is necessary.

Clean the refrigerator regularly, using a specially formulated germicidal refrigerator cleaner. Alternatively, use a weak solution of bicarbonate of soda: 1 tbsp to 1 litre (1$\frac{3}{4}$ pints) water.

If your refrigerator doesn't have an automatic defrost facility, defrost regularly.

Maximum refrigerator storage times

For pre-packed foods, always adhere to the 'use by' date on the packet. For other foods the following storage times should apply, providing the food is in prime condition when it goes into the refrigerator and that your refrigerator is in good working order.

Vegetables and Fruit

Green vegetables	3–4 days
Salad leaves	2–3 days
Hard and stone fruit	3–7 days
Soft fruit	1–2 days

Dairy Food

Cheese, hard	1 week
Cheese, soft	2–3 days
Eggs	1 week
Milk	4–5 days

Fish

Fish	1 day
Shellfish	1 day

Raw Meat

Bacon	7 days
Minced meat	1 day
Poultry	2 days
Raw sliced meat	2 days
Sausages	3 days

Cooked Meat

Pies	2 days
Sliced meat	2 days
Ham	2 days
Ham, vacuum-packed (or according to the instructions on the packet)	1–2 weeks

1

Birthday Cakes

Cook's Tip

If you are particularly artistic, finish off the cake by drawing a design on the icing to make it look like wrapping paper. The simplest way to do this is to use edible food colouring pens. These are available from specialist kitchen shops, and look just like felt-tips. You can also use them to write a message on the tag.

Birthday Parcel Cake

butter to grease

1 x 4-egg quantity of Victoria sponge mixture (see page 17)

1 x quantity of buttercream icing (see page 22)

For the icing

450g (1lb) white ready-to-roll icing (sugar paste)

200g (7oz) ready-made marzipan or ready-to-roll icing (sugar paste)

red and green food colourings

icing sugar to dust

1 medium egg white, lightly beaten

1 Grease and line two 18cm (7in) square cake tins. Make the sponge mixture according to the instructions on page 16, divide between the tins and bake. Leave on a wire rack until cold.

2 Sandwich the cold cakes together with all but 2 tbsp of the buttercream. Put the cake on a plate or cake board and spread the reserved buttercream smoothly over the top and sides. Set aside.

3 Knead the 450g (1lb) icing until pliable. Put a small amount aside for the gift tag and thread, then roll out the remainder to a 30.5cm (12in) square. Place over the cake and trim small triangles out of the corners to avoid excess icing. Smooth over the joins.

4 For the decoration, knead the marzipan or icing until pliable. Divide into two pieces weighing 125g (4oz) and 75g (3oz). Knead a few drops of red food colouring into the larger piece until evenly coloured; knead the green colouring into the smaller piece.

5 Lightly dust the worksurface with icing sugar. Roll out the green marzipan or icing and cut into two strips each measuring 30.5 x 2.5cm (12 x 1in). Then roll out the red marzipan or icing and cut into two strips measuring 12.5 x 2cm (5 x 3/4in); one strip measuring 7.5 x 2cm (3 x 3/4in); two strips measuring 5 x 2cm (2 x 3/4in). Set aside.

6 Brush one side of the green strips with a little of the beaten egg white, then place them, moistened-side down, on top of the cake (in an off-centre cross) to look like ribbon on a parcel. Mark the edges of the ribbon with a fork.

7 Loop the two 12.5cm (5in) red strips to look like a bow and fix on top of the cake with egg white. Cut the 7.5cm (3in) and one of the 5cm (2in) strips in a V-shape to form the ends of the ribbon. Fix in place with egg white.

8 Use the remaining 5cm (2in) red strip to form the centre of the bow. If you like, use the reserved icing to make a tag and thread, then fix on the cake. Leave overnight to dry out and set.

Serves	A LITTLE EFFORT		NUTRITIONAL INFORMATION	
10	**Preparation Time** 1 hour	**Cooking Time** 25–30 minutes, plus cooling and drying	**Per Serving** 586 calories, 17.7g fat (of which 9.1g saturates), 105.4g carbohydrate, 0.5g salt	Vegetarian

Cook's Tip

Lightly whip 300ml (½ pint) whipping cream and use to sandwich the meringues together.

Pastel Meringues

4 large egg whites

250g (9oz) icing sugar, sifted

1 tsp vanilla extract

red or pink food colouring

edible silver or pink balls to decorate

novelty candles to decorate (optional)

1 Preheat the oven to 130°C (110°C fan oven) mark ½. Line two or three baking trays with baking parchment.

2 Put the egg whites in a clean, grease-free bowl of a freestanding mixer and whisk until stiff (or use an electric hand whisk if you prefer). Add the sugar, 1 tbsp at a time, whisking well between additions, to make a stiff, glossy meringue. The mixture shouldn't move around in the bowl. Whisk in the vanilla extract.

3 Add 1–2 drops of red or pink food colouring, one drop at a time. Mix well until you have a pastel pink colour.

4 To make oval-shaped meringues, use two dessertspoons. Take a spoonful of mixture in one spoon and use the other spoon to scrape the meringue away from you on to the parchment. Sprinkle with the silver or pink balls.

5 Bake for 1 hour, turn off the heat and leave in the oven for 1–1½ hours to dry out. Remove from the oven and cool on a wire rack.

6 Pile up on a plate into a tower shape and insert novelty candles to decorate.

Serves 10	EASY		NUTRITIONAL INFORMATION	
	Preparation Time 30 minutes	**Cooking Time** 1 hour, plus drying	**Per Serving** 103 calories, 0g fat (of which 0g saturates), 26.1g carbohydrate, 0.1g salt	Vegetarian Gluten free • Dairy free

Cook's Tip

To melt chocolate, put it in a heatproof bowl set over a pan of gently simmering water and leave until melted. Stir until smooth.

Gluten-free Chocolate Cake

125g (4oz) butter, softened, plus extra to grease

200g (7oz) light muscovado sugar

2 large eggs, lightly beaten

125g (4oz) gluten-free plain chocolate, broken into pieces, melted (see Cook's Tip) and left to cool slightly

100g (3½oz) natural yogurt

few drops of vanilla extract

200g (7oz) brown rice flour

½ tsp wheat-free baking powder

1 tsp bicarbonate of soda

For the icing

150g (5oz) gluten-free plain chocolate, broken into pieces

150ml (¼ pint) double cream

large milk and plain or white chocolate buttons (gluten-free) to decorate

1 Preheat the oven to 180°C (160°C fan oven) mark 4. Grease a deep 18cm (7in) square cake tin and line with greaseproof paper.

2 Cream the butter and sugar together until light and fluffy. Gradually beat in the eggs, then the melted chocolate, yogurt and vanilla extract. Sift together the rice flour, baking powder and bicarbonate of soda. Beat into the mixture a little at a time. Pour into the prepared tin and bake for 45 minutes–1 hour or until a skewer inserted in the centre comes out clean. Leave to cool in the tin for 10 minutes, then transfer to a wire rack to cool completely.

3 To make the icing, put the chocolate in a heatproof bowl. Heat the cream to just below boiling point. Pour on to the chocolate. Leave for 5 minutes, then beat until the chocolate has melted and the mixture is smooth. Cool until thickened, then spread all over the cake with a palette knife. Decorate the top and sides with alternate milk and plain or white chocolate buttons to create a polka-dot effect.

EASY		NUTRITIONAL INFORMATION		Serves
Preparation Time 30 minutes	**Cooking Time** 45 minutes–1 hour, plus cooling	**Per Serving** 476 calories, 27.7g fat (of which 16.3g saturates), 55.9g carbohydrate, 0.3g salt	Vegetarian Gluten free	**10**

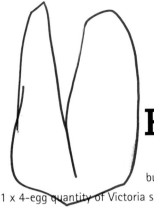

Happy Birthday Cake

butter to grease

1 x 4-egg quantity of Victoria sponge mixture
(see page 17)

1 x quantity of buttercream icing (see page 22)

900g (2lb) white marzipan or ready-to-roll icing
(sugar paste)

red, blue and green food colourings

gold stars to decorate (optional)

1 Grease and line two 18cm (7in) square cake tins. Make the sponge mixture according to the instructions on page 16, divide between the tins and bake. Leave on a wire rack until cold.

2 Sandwich the cold cakes together with all but 2 tbsp of the buttercream. Put the cake on a cake board and spread the reserved buttercream smoothly over the top and sides. Set aside.

3 Cut off one-third of the marzipan or icing and roll out thinly to fit the top of the cake. Cut to size and put to one side. Knead the trimmings together with the remaining marzipan or icing.

4 Divide the remaining marzipan or icing into three pieces and colour each piece red, blue and green respectively. Roll out each piece thinly and cut into an oblong measuring 18 x 10cm (7 x 4in). Knead the trimmings together, keeping the colours separate.

5 Cut each coloured oblong into strips measuring 18 x 2cm (7 x ³/₄in). Separate the strips and lay two strips of different colours alongside each other on the worksurface, to fit the depth of one side of the cake. Lightly roll the strips together to join them, keeping them straight. Run a palette knife underneath the strips to ensure that they move freely.

6 Stick the joined strips along one side of the cake and trim to fit. Repeat on each side of the cake. Position the white square of marzipan or icing on top of the cake. Cut the remaining coloured strips into 1cm (¹/₂in) widths and position around the top of the cake.

7 Roll out the trimmings of marzipan or icing thinly. Using small alphabet cutters, cut out letters to make 'Happy Birthday' and arrange in the centre of the cake – brush the backs of the letters with a little water to stick down. Mould any remaining trimmings into balloon shapes with strings and arrange them on top of the cake. Leave to dry in a cool place. Add gold stars, if using.

Cook's Tips

Cut the marzipan or icing strips with a wet knife to obtain clean-cut strips.

If the top of the cake is not level, invert the cake before decorating it.

Gold stars aren't edible, so remove them before slicing.

A LITTLE EFFORT		NUTRITIONAL INFORMATION		Serves
Preparation Time 1 hour	**Cooking Time** 25 minutes, plus cooling and drying	**Per Serving** 711 calories, 26.6g fat (of which 9.9g saturates), 111.5g carbohydrate, 0.5g salt	Vegetarian	**10**

Try Something Different

Soften the ice cream for 10 minutes and stir in half the marshmallows. Return to the freezer until ready to assemble the meringue.

Get Ahead

To prepare ahead Complete the recipe to the end of step 2. Cool completely, then store the meringues in an airtight tin for up to two weeks.
To use Complete the recipe.

Marshmallow Meringue Cake

6 large egg whites

350g (12oz) golden caster sugar

1 tsp cornflour

½ tsp white vinegar

For the filling

vanilla or chocolate-chip ice cream

4 bananas, about 450g (1lb)

mini marshmallows

For the decoration

chocolate sprinkles or grated chocolate

flaked almonds, toasted

icing sugar or cocoa to dust

1 Preheat the oven to 130°C (110°C fan oven) mark ½. Line two baking sheets with baking parchment. Mark out a circle, 23cm (9in) in diameter, on each piece of baking parchment and turn the paper over.

2 Whisk the egg whites in a clean, grease-free bowl until stiff and dry. Whisk in the sugar, 1 tbsp at a time, until the mixture is glossy and very stiff, then whisk in the cornflour and vinegar. Spoon just under half the meringue on to one circle of parchment to form a ring shape. Spread the remaining mixture evenly over the other circle to cover it completely. Bake for 2–2½ hours, then turn off the oven and leave the meringues inside to cool for 30 minutes. Remove from the oven and leave to cool completely.

3 About 30 minutes before serving, take the ice cream from the freezer. Put the meringue circle on a plate. Slice the bananas and scatter over the meringue with some marshmallows. Put ice cream scoops and more marshmallows on top. Add the meringue ring and scatter with sprinkles, almonds and cocoa.

Serves 10	EASY		NUTRITIONAL INFORMATION	
	Preparation Time 45 minutes, plus 30 minutes softening	**Cooking Time** 2½ hours, plus cooling	**Per Serving** 536 calories, 1.7g fat (of which 1g saturates), 131.8g carbohydrate, 0.2g salt	Gluten free

Hickory Dickory Dock Cake

butter to grease
1 x 3-egg quantity of Victoria sponge mixture
(see page 17)
1 x quantity of buttercream icing (see page 22)
450g (1lb) white ready-to-roll icing (sugar paste)
blue food colouring
small sugar mouse or toy mouse to decorate
coloured ribbon

1 Grease and line two 18cm (7in) round cake tins. Make the sponge mixture according to the instructions on page 16, divide between the tins and bake. Leave on a wire rack until cold.

2 Sandwich the cold cakes together with all but 2 tbsp of the buttercream. Put the cake on a plate or cake board and spread the reserved buttercream smoothly over the top and sides (reserving a tiny amount of buttercream to stick the sugar mouse). Set aside.

3 Cut off 100g (3½oz) of the ready-to-roll icing and set aside; roll out the rest thinly and cover the cake, smoothing out any creases with your hands as you go. Trim away the icing around the base of the cake and reserve the trimmings.

4 Knead the remaining icing with the trimmings and a few drops of food colouring. Roll out thinly. Cut out two strips, measuring half the diameter of the cake, to make the hands of the clock. Trim one end of each hand into an arrow shape, and shorten one piece to form the little hand. Use the offcut to cut out a circular pivot for the ends of the hands. Cut out the numbers one to 12 with small number cutters.

5 Brush the backs of the numbers with water and arrange on the cake to resemble a clock face. Fix on the hands of the clock in the same way, setting them at one o'clock. Stick the sugar mouse, if using, on the face of the clock with a dot of the reserved buttercream, or put the toy mouse in position. Tie a ribbon around the cake.

EASY		NUTRITIONAL INFORMATION		Serves
Preparation Time 45 minutes	**Cooking Time** 20–25 minutes, plus cooling	**Per Serving** 455 calories, 12.1g fat (of which 7g saturates), 86.7g carbohydrate, 0.3g salt	Vegetarian	**10**

Alphabet Carrot Tray Bake

butter to grease

275g (10oz) self-raising flour

350g (12oz) caster sugar

2 tsp baking powder and 3 tsp mixed spice

300ml (½ pint) sunflower oil

4 medium eggs

1 tsp vanilla extract

275g (10oz) carrots, peeled and grated

For the decoration

about 6 tbsp apricot glaze (see page 19)

icing sugar to dust

750g (1lb 11oz) white ready-to-roll icing (sugar paste)

assorted food colourings

coloured ribbon

1 Preheat the oven to 180°C (160°C fan oven) mark 4. Grease and line a 30.5 x 23cm (12 x 9in) roasting tin.

2 Put the flour, sugar, baking powder and spice into a large bowl. Whisk together the oil, eggs and vanilla extract in a jug and stir into the flour mix. Stir in the grated carrots, then turn into the roasting tin. Bake for 50–60 minutes until the cake is golden brown and firm when pressed with your fingertips. Cool in the tin for 10 minutes, then turn out on to a wire rack to cool completely.

3 Trim the edges of the cake to neaten. Put on a cake board. Brush the sides and top with the apricot glaze. Dust a worksurface lightly with icing sugar, roll out two-thirds of the icing, then lay the icing over the cake. Smooth over the top and down the sides and cut away any excess with a sharp knife.

4 Knead the trimmings with the remaining icing. Divide into three and colour each with a different food colouring. Roll out thinly and use cutters to cut out alphabet shapes. Brush the backs of the shapes with water and stick randomly across the top of the cake. Tie a ribbon around the cake.

Serves 21	EASY		NUTRITIONAL INFORMATION	
	Preparation Time 45 minutes	**Cooking Time** 50 minutes–1 hour, plus cooling	**Per Serving** 352 calories, 12g fat (of which 1.6g saturates), 61.7g carbohydrate, 0.2g salt	Dairy free

Banana and Chocolate Ice Cream Pie

500ml tub chocolate ice cream

75g (3oz) butter, plus extra to grease

200g (7oz) plain chocolate digestive biscuits

2 large bananas, sliced

juice of ½ lemon

1 king-size Mars Bar, cut into thin slivers and chilled

1 Take the ice cream out of the freezer to let it soften. Grease a 20.5cm (8in) loose-based, fluted flan tin and line the base with greaseproof paper. Put the butter in a small pan and melt over a medium heat.

2 Put the biscuits into a food processor and whizz until they resemble coarse breadcrumbs. Alternatively, put them in a plastic bag and crush with a rolling pin. Transfer to a bowl. Pour the melted butter into the processor and blend with the biscuits to combine, or stir into the crushed crumbs until well combined. Press into the base of the prepared tin.

3 Toss the bananas in the lemon juice and scatter over the base. Upturn the ice cream tub on to the bananas and use a palette knife to spread the ice cream evenly, covering the fruit.

4 Scatter the Mars Bar slices over the ice cream and freeze for at least 1 hour before slicing to serve.

EASY	NUTRITIONAL INFORMATION		Serves
Preparation Time 15 minutes, plus 1 hour freezing	**Per Serving** 406 calories, 25.6g fat (of which 15.1g saturates), 42.2g carbohydrate, 0.6g salt	Vegetarian	**8**

Try Something Different

Adjust the decoration to suit the age of the kids

Chocolate Crown

butter to grease

1 x 3-egg quantity of chocolate Victoria sponge mixture
(see page 17)

1 x quantity of buttercream icing (see page 22)

For the chocolate crown

250g (9oz) good-quality white chocolate,
broken into pieces

8 white chocolate buttons

jelly sweets and edible silver and pink balls

assorted sweets for the centre decoration

1 Grease and line two 18cm (7in) round cake tins. Make the sponge mixture according to the instructions on page 16, divide between the tins and bake. Leave on a wire rack until cold.

2 Sandwich the cold cakes together with all but 2 tbsp of the buttercream. Put the cake on a plate or cake board and spread the reserved buttercream smoothly over the top and sides. Set aside.

3 To make the crown, melt the chocolate in a heatproof bowl over a pan of gently simmering water; set aside. Measure the exact circumference of the cake with a piece of string. Cut two strips of greaseproof paper the same length as the string and 10cm (4in) wide. Fold one paper strip in half, then in half twice more to make a rectangle of eight thicknesses. Using a

pencil, draw a curve between the two folded points, then cut along the curve through all thicknesses. Open out the paper to reveal the fluted edge and lay on top of the second paper strip. Draw around the fluted outline on the second paper strip to make the template for the crown, then turn over and discard the cut strip.

4 With a palette knife, carefully spread the melted chocolate within the template and up to the edges (reserve 1–2 tbsp for fixing on decorations and put into a small paper piping bag). Leave until the chocolate has set just enough for it not to run when you pick up the paper.

5 Carefully lift the paper strip by the uncoated areas, and position around the cake so the chocolate rests against the side of the cake and the ends of the strip just meet. Chill or leave in a cool place until the chocolate has set.

6 When cold, carefully peel away the greaseproof paper, leaving the chocolate crown in position. Pipe a dot of melted chocolate on each of the points of the crown and gently secure a chocolate button on each. Pipe dots around the crown and stick on jelly sweets for jewels. (If the chocolate has set in the piping bag, soften in the microwave on Defrost for up to 1 minute, checking frequently.) Press the silver balls into the crown. Store in a cool place. When ready to serve, pile the assorted sweets on top of the cake.

Serves 12	A LITTLE EFFORT		NUTRITIONAL INFORMATION	
	Preparation Time 45 minutes	**Cooking Time** 25 minutes, plus cooling and setting	**Per Serving** 358 calories, 16.5g fat (of which 9.7g saturates), 50.1g carbohydrate, 0.3g salt	Vegetarian

Egg-free Chocolate Cake

150ml (¼ pint) sunflower oil, plus extra to grease
75g (3oz) creamed coconut
25g (1oz) plain chocolate, in pieces
50g (2oz) cocoa powder
350g (12oz) self-raising flour
1 tsp baking powder
pinch of salt
175g (6oz) light muscovado sugar

For the icing

350g (12oz) plain chocolate, broken into small pieces
150ml (¼ pint) double cream
white and milk chocolate Maltesers to decorate

1 Preheat the oven to 180°C (160°C fan oven) mark 4. Grease and line a 1.7 litre (3 pint) loaf tin measuring 30.5 x 10cm (12 x 4in).

2 Put the creamed coconut in a heatproof bowl, pour on 425ml (14fl oz) boiling water and stir to dissolve. Set aside to cool for 30 minutes.

3 Melt the chocolate in a heatproof bowl over a pan of gently simmering water. Stir until smooth and leave to cool slightly.

4 Sift the cocoa, flour, baking powder and salt into a bowl. Stir in the sugar and make a well in the middle. Add the coconut mixture, melted chocolate and sunflower oil. Beat to make a smooth batter.

5 Pour the cake batter into the tin. Bake for 1–1¼ hours or until risen and just firm to the touch, covering with foil after about 40 minutes if it gets too brown on top. Leave in the tin for 10 minutes, then transfer to a wire rack to cool. When cold, trim to neaten the edges.

6 To make the icing, put the chocolate in a heatproof bowl. Heat the cream to just below boiling point. Pour on to the chocolate and stir until melted. Leave to cool, beating occasionally, until thick – pop into the refrigerator for 30 minutes to help thicken if necessary.

7 Cut the cake in half horizontally and sandwich the layers together with one-third of the icing. Spread the rest evenly over the top and sides of the cake. Decorate the top of the cake with alternate rows of milk and white Maltesers. Decorate the bottom of the cake with an edging of alternate milk and white Maltesers.

Serves	EASY		NUTRITIONAL INFORMATION	
12	**Preparation Time** 30 minutes, plus 30 minutes soaking	**Cooking Time** 1–1¼ hours, plus cooling	**Per Serving** 515 calories, 31g fat (of which 14.5g saturates), 58.8g carbohydrate, 0.4g salt	Vegetarian

Cook's Tip

If time is really short, substitute a couple of good shop-bought Madeira cakes for the cake mixture. Most supermarkets sell family-sized versions, which you can cut to the size you need and spread with the buttercream.

Try Something Different

Adapt this simple cake to suit any theme. Colour the icing according to whether you want grass for a football pitch, sand for a beach, or soil for a farm, and decorate with plastic figurines and coloured decorations.

Large Marbled Birthday Cake

350g (12oz) very soft butter, plus extra to grease
350g (12oz) caster sugar
450g (1lb) self-raising flour, sifted
3 tsp baking powder
6 medium eggs
6 tbsp milk
2 tsp vanilla extract
pink food colouring (or any other colour you like)
4 tbsp cocoa powder blended with a little hot water and cooled

For the decoration

2 x 325g tubs ready-made vanilla buttercream icing
pink or red food colouring
writing icing
pink and white sugar flowers
butterfly decorations (optional)

1 Preheat the oven to 180°C (160°C fan oven) mark 4. Grease and line a 29 x 36cm (11½ x 14½in) roasting tin or the nearest equivalent.

2 Put the butter, sugar, flour, baking powder, eggs, milk and vanilla extract into a bowl. Beat with an electric hand whisk for 2 minutes until smooth.

3 Put about one-third of the cake mixture in a bowl, add a few drops of the food colouring and beat in. Put another third of the mixture in another bowl and add the cocoa powder and a little more milk if necessary. Mix well.

4 Put a dollop of plain cake mixture in the cake tin, then add a spoonful of chocolate mixture, followed by a spoonful of coloured mixture. Keep doing this until all the cake mixtures are in the tin.

5 Briefly swirl a skewer or knife through the mixture to give a marbled effect. Level the surface of the mixture and bake for about 40–45 minutes or until the cake has shrunk away from the sides of the tin and springs back when pressed in the centre with your fingertips. Leave to cool in the tin.

6 Turn out the cake on to a worksurface and trim the edges to neaten. Place on a cake board with the smooth side uppermost. Tip the buttercream into a large bowl and mix in a few drops of food colouring until it is pale pink. Spread over the top and sides of the cake. Write your birthday message in the centre with the writing icing, then decorate with the sugar flowers. Fix in the butterflies, if using (remove these before you cut the cake).

EASY		NUTRITIONAL INFORMATION		Serves
Preparation Time 40 minutes	**Cooking Time** 40–45 minutes, plus cooling	**Per Serving** 534 calories, 26.4g fat (of which 16.7g saturates), 75.6g carbohydrate, 0.6g salt	Vegetarian	**32**

2

Themed Cakes

Creepy-crawly Cake

butter to grease

1 x 4-egg quantity of chocolate Victoria sponge mixture
(see page 17)

½ quantity of chocolate buttercream icing (see page 22)

For the decoration

225g (8oz) white ready-to-roll icing (sugar paste)

assorted food colourings, including black and brown

red and black liquorice bootlaces and jelly creepy-crawly
sweets, such as snakes and frogs

a little glacé icing (see page 22)

For the icing

450g (1lb) icing sugar, sifted

225g (8oz) butter, softened

few drops of vanilla extract

green food colouring

1 To make a trap door, use 125g (4oz) ready-to-roll icing. Knead in a few drops of brown food colouring and roll out to a thickness of 5mm (¼in), then use a small tumbler to cut out a circle. Place on a baking tray lined with non-stick baking parchment and leave in a cool place overnight to dry.

2 Use the remaining white and brown icing to make a selection of spiders and beetles, colouring the icing accordingly. Use the liquorice to make spiders' legs. Pipe eyes on to the creatures with white glacé icing. Allow to dry overnight.

3 Next day, grease and line two 20.5cm (8in) round sandwich tins. Make the sponge mixture according to the instructions on page 16, divide between the tins and bake. Leave to cool, then sandwich with chocolate buttercream. Cut out a hole 1cm (½in) deep and 6.5cm (2½in) wide in the centre of the cake. Discard (or eat) the trimmings.

4 To make the icing, beat the icing sugar into the butter with the vanilla. Beat in the food colouring.

5 Put the cake on a board or plate and cover with the green icing. Secure the trap door over the hole in the middle of the cake and prop open with a cocktail stick painted with brown food colouring, or a chocolate matchstick. Arrange the creatures over the cake. Make sure that some creepy-crawlies are crawling out of the trap door. Leave to dry.

Serves	A LITTLE EFFORT		NUTRITIONAL INFORMATION	
12–15	**Preparation Time** 1½ hours plus overnight drying	**Cooking Time** 25–30 minutes, plus cooling	**Per Serving** 534 calories, 26.4 fat (of which 16.7g saturates), 75.6g carbohydrate, 0.6g salt	Vegetarian

Cook's Tip

To save time, this can be made from shop-bought cakes.

Sleeping Beauty's Castle

1 x white ready-iced square 23cm (9in)
sponge cake

5 raspberry or strawberry Swiss rolls, about 9cm (3½in) long

450g (1lb) white ready-to-roll icing (sugar paste)

icing sugar to dust

apricot glaze (see page 19)

1 x white ready-iced round 15cm (6in) sponge cake

2 x quantity of pink buttercream icing (see page 22)

5 ice cream sugar cones

For the decoration

multi-coloured sprinkles

red, pink, yellow, green and white writing icing

sugar flowers

paper flag

small pink round sweets or pink edible balls

1 Put the square cake on a 30.5cm (12in) square cake board. Measure the circumference of a Swiss roll with a piece of string. Divide the ready-to-roll icing into five pieces. Lightly dust a worksurface with icing sugar, then roll out each piece of icing thinly into a rectangle the length of the Swiss roll by the length of the piece of string. Neaten the edges with a sharp knife. Brush each piece of icing with apricot glaze and roll around a Swiss roll, gently working the edges together to seal.

2 Put the round cake in the centre of the square cake. Put a dollop of buttercream at each corner of the square cake and position four of the Swiss rolls, with the sealed edge facing inwards, to make towers. Smooth pink buttercream over four of the cones and spread a little on top of each tower. Dip the tips of the cones in sprinkles, then fix on top of the towers. Using red writing icing, draw a simple window, divided by four panes, at the top of each tower.

3 At the front of the castle, use red writing icing to draw a door with a doorknob. Use pink and yellow writing icing to draw small flowers around the castle and below the windows. Fix a few sugar flowers to the walls with writing icing. Connect the flowers with green writing icing to represent stems. Use the green icing to draw clumps of grass around the base of the wall. Stick a sugar flower to the paper flag with writing icing.

4 Position the remaining Swiss roll in the centre of the round cake. Cover the remaining cone with buttercream, drip in sprinkles and position on top of the round cake, fixing with a little buttercream. Draw on windows and decorate with sugar flowers as before. Make blobs of white writing icing, just touching each other, around the edges of the cones and decorate with pink sweets or edible balls. Stick the paper flag into the central tower.

EASY	NUTRITIONAL INFORMATION		Serves
Preparation Time 1 hour	**Per Serving** 425 calories, 8.1g fat (of which 2.5g saturates), 85.5g carbohydrate, 0.2g salt	Vegetarian	**35**

Cook's Tip

If you prefer, make just one of the creatures and multiply the relevant icing ingredients by three.

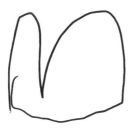

Hedgehogs, Ladybirds and Tortoises

50g (2oz) butter, plus extra to grease

50g (2oz) caster sugar

1 medium egg, beaten

50g (2oz) self-raising flour

1 tbsp milk

1 x quantity of chocolate buttercream icing (see page 22)

75g (3oz) red ready-to-roll icing (sugar paste)

black and brown writing icing

125g (4oz) green ready-to-roll icing (sugar paste)

50g (2oz) brown ready-to-roll icing (sugar paste)

apricot jam

For the decoration

chocolate sprinkles and milk and white chocolate drops

edible silver or gold balls

dolly mixture sweets

1 Preheat the oven to 180°C (160°C fan oven) mark 4. Cream the butter and sugar together until light and fluffy. Gradually beat in the egg. Fold in the flour and milk. Divide the mixture among 15 holes of well-greased bun tins (with rounded bases). Bake in the oven for about 15 minutes. Cool on a wire rack.

2 Make the hedgehogs. Cover five of the cold buns with chocolate buttercream, shaping to form a snout. Decorate with chocolate sprinkles, silver or gold balls for eyes and a dolly mixture sweet for the nose.

3 Make the ladybirds. Roll out the red icing thinly and use to cover a further five buns. Using black writing icing, pipe wings, spots and a smile on the ladybirds and use chocolate drops for eyes.

4 Make the tortoises. Cover the remaining buns with green icing. Use brown writing icing to draw 'shell' markings and add white chocolate drops. Make the heads, legs and tails from brown icing, and attach to the body with a little jam. Add silver balls for eyes.

Serves 15	A LITTLE EFFORT		NUTRITIONAL INFORMATION	
	Preparation Time 1 hour	**Cooking Time** 15 minutes, plus cooling	**Per Serving** 178 calories, 3.5g fat (of which 2g saturates), 37.1g carbohydrate, 0.1g salt	Vegetarian

Cook's Tip

To make the templates for the house you will need the following card shapes:
roof: 10 x 6.5cm (4 x 2¹/₂in)
long side wall: 10 x 6cm (4 x 2¹/₄in)
end wall: 6 x 8cm (2¹/₄ x 3¹/₄in)

Gingerbread House

150g (5oz) butter, plus extra to grease
350g (12oz) plain white flour, sifted
1 tsp bicarbonate of soda
2 tbsp ground ginger
200g (7oz) light muscovado sugar
2 tbsp golden syrup
1 medium egg, beaten

For the decoration

200g (7oz) icing sugar, sifted
1 medium egg white
75g (3oz) assorted sweets
4 x 15cm (6in) cake boards covered in paper

1 Grease two baking sheets. Put the flour, bicarbonate of soda and ginger into a bowl. Rub in the butter until the mixture resembles breadcrumbs. Stir in the sugar. Warm the golden syrup in a pan, pour on to the flour with the beaten egg and stir. Bring together into a soft dough; knead until smooth. Divide into four, wrap in clingfilm and chill for 15 minutes.

2 Roll out one piece of dough to 3mm (¹/₄in) thick. Cut out two of each template (see Cook's Tip). Put on to the baking sheets. Repeat with the remaining dough to make the pieces for the other three gingerbread houses. Chill for 15 minutes. Preheat the oven to 190°C (170°C fan oven) mark 5. Bake for 8–10 minutes until golden. Leave on the baking sheets for 5 minutes, then transfer to a wire rack until cold.

3 To decorate, beat the icing sugar into the egg white until the mixture stands in peaks. Spoon into a piping bag and pipe windows and doors on the walls and squiggly lines on the roof. Leave to dry for 2 hours. Pipe icing along the edge of the side walls and stick to the end walls. Leave to dry for 1 hour, then place on a board and fill with sweets. Pipe icing along the top of each house and the roof pieces and press gently in position; hold for 1–2 minutes until secure. Leave to set for at least 2 hours.

A LITTLE EFFORT		NUTRITIONAL INFORMATION		Makes
Preparation Time 4 hours	**Cooking Time** 10 minutes, plus chilling and drying	**Per House** 1,000 calories, 34g fat (of which 21g saturates), 198g carbohydrate, 0.9g salt	Vegetarian	**4** houses

Clown Cake

25g (1oz) each of white, green, black and blue
ready-to-roll icing (sugar paste)
50g (2oz) red ready-to-roll icing (sugar paste)
black and yellow writing icing
1 x white ready-iced 20.5cm (8in) sponge cake

1 First make the shapes for the clown's face. Roll out the white ready-to-roll icing and cut out two ovals for eyes. Roll out half the red icing and cut out a crescent shape for the mouth. Mark a smiley line along the centre of the mouth with black writing icing. Knead the trimmings and the other piece of red icing together and roll into a ball for his nose. Roll out a small piece of green icing and, using a star-shaped cutter, stamp out two stars for his cheeks.

2 Brush the backs of the shapes with water and position on the cake. Roll out the black icing and cut out two small circles to make pupils for the eyes; stick on to the white ovals. Use the black and yellow writing icing to give him eyebrows and a swirl of hair.

3 Roll out the blue icing and cut out two sides of a bow tie. Roll the trimmings into a ball and flatten slightly to make the centre knot. Fix the two bow-tie pieces to the bottom edge of the cake with writing icing. Position the knot on top. Use the yellow writing icing to pipe polka dots on the tie.

EASY	NUTRITIONAL INFORMATION	Serves
Preparation Time 45 minutes	**Per Serving** 300 calories, 7.6g fat (of which 2.2g saturates), 55g carbohydrate, 0.1g salt Vegetarian	**15**

Cook's Tip

Save time and buy plastic ballet shoes for decoration from supermarkets or specialist cake decorating shops.

Try Something Different

For a football theme, replace the ballet shoes with a miniature pair of plastic football boots and ice the cake with the relevant team colours.

Ballet Shoe Cake

butter to grease

1 x 4-egg quantity of lemon Victoria sponge mixture
(see page 17)

good-quality lemon curd for filling

apricot glaze (see page 19)

700g (1½lb) white ready-to-roll icing (sugar paste)

red or pink food colouring

icing sugar to dust

For the decoration

½ quantity of royal icing (see page 22), coloured
deep pink

sugar flowers and edible silver balls

pink ribbon

1 Grease and line two 20.5cm (8in) round sandwich tins. Make the sponge mixture according to the instructions on page 16, divide between the tins and bake. Leave to cool, then sandwich together with the lemon curd. Brush the cake with apricot glaze.

2 Set aside a small piece of the ready-to-roll icing to make the ballet shoes. Knead a few drops of the red or pink food colouring into the remaining icing to make it pale pink. Dust a worksurface lightly with icing sugar and roll out the icing to make a circle 5cm (2in) bigger than the top of the cake. Cover the cake with the icing, smoothing it out evenly across the top and down the sides, using your hand. Trim away any excess from the base.

3 Make a pair of ballet shoes using the reserved icing. Position the ballet shoes at the top of the cake and stick in place with a dab of royal icing. Pipe scrolls (elongated S-shapes) around the cake, and fix the sugar flowers in between with a dot of icing. Decorate the scrolls and flowers with silver balls. For a finishing touch, tie a ribbon around the cake.

Serves	A LITTLE EFFORT		NUTRITIONAL INFORMATION	
12–15	**Preparation Time** 45 minutes	**Cooking Time** 25–30 minutes, plus cooling	**Per Serving** 410 calories, 10g fat (of which 6g saturates), 82g carbohydrate, 0.5g salt	Vegetarian

Space Rocket Cake

black food colouring

900g (2lb) white ready-to-roll icing (sugar paste)

icing sugar to dust

1 ready-made Madeira cake slab

apricot glaze (see page 19)

ice cream sugar cone

6 chocolate mini rolls

6 candles with holders

red and black writing icing

edible silver balls to decorate

1 First, make the surface of the moon. Knead a few drops of black food colouring into half the ready-to-roll icing to make a grey, lunar-like colour. Roll out a square of grey icing to fit a 30.5cm (12in) cake board, but first, stick pieces of grey icing on the board to make rocks, and press some in the centre so that they look like craters. Lay the circle of grey icing over the rocks and craters and smooth to fit.

2 To make the spaceship, dust a worksurface lightly with icing sugar and roll out three-quarters of the remaining white icing thinly. Brush the Madeira cake with apricot glaze and stick the sugar cone to one of the short ends with more glaze. Lay the white icing over the top and mould around the shape, smoothing it with your hands and tucking the joins underneath. Fix on the lunar board with a dab of apricot glaze.

3 Slice one end off each mini roll so that you can see the icing inside. Stack up into a pyramid shape. Roll out the remaining white icing into a strip and neaten the edges with a sharp knife. Wrap around the pyramid, moulding gently as you go. Leave the ends of the rolls exposed and insert candles in holders as shown. Put against the bottom of the spaceship, fixing with apricot glaze.

4 With black writing icing, write 'NASA 69' (or appropriate year) and mark panels on the body of the rocket. Decorate with silver balls. Use red writing icing to draw stripes over the engine section.

Serves	EASY	NUTRITIONAL INFORMATION	
6	**Preparation Time** 40 minutes	**Per Serving** 1010 calories, 26g fat (of which 15g saturates), 192g carbohydrate, 0.7g salt	Vegetarian

1 x 4-egg quantity of chocolate Victoria sponge mixture (see page 17)

1 x 3-egg quantity of chocolate Victoria sponge mixture (see page 17)

2 x quantities of chocolate buttercream icing (see page 22)

white writing icing

milk chocolate matchsticks

paper flags attached to cocktail sticks

Knight's Castle

1 Make and bake the four-egg cake in a 20.5cm (8in) square tin, and the three-egg cake in an 18cm (7in) square tin, according to the instructions on pages 16–17. Leave on a wire rack until cold.

2 Trim the top of the large cake to make it flat. Place the cake, cut-side down, in the centre of a plate or 30.5cm (12in) cake board. Cover the large cake with two-thirds of the chocolate buttercream. Neaten the edges of the smaller cake and cut into nine equal squares. To form a tower, put two squares on top of each other, sandwiched with buttercream, at one corner of the large cake; secure with a cocktail stick. Cover with chocolate buttercream. Repeat with the remaining squares in the other three corners of the cake (you'll have one square left over, which you can discard or eat).

3 With the white writing icing, draw arrow slits on each tower. In the centre of the main facing wall, stick a row of chocolate sticks to make a drawbridge. Stick the flags into each tower.

A LITTLE EFFORT		NUTRITIONAL INFORMATION		Serves
Preparation Time 1 hour	**Cooking Time** 45 minutes, plus cooling	**Per Serving** 258 calories, 10.9g fat (of which 6.3g saturates), 38.4g carbohydrate, 0.4g salt	Vegetarian	**25**

Toadstool

butter to grease

1 x quantity of 3-egg Victoria sponge mixture
(see page 17)

700g (1½lb) white ready-to-roll icing (sugar paste)

brown, red, green and yellow food colourings

½ quantity of buttercream icing (see page 22)

cornflour to dust

sugar flowers, dolly mixtures and butterfly decorations

1 Preheat the oven to 190°C (170°C fan oven) mark 5. Grease and base-line a 900g (2lb) food can and a 1.1 litre (2 pint) pudding basin. It doesn't matter how big the basin is, as long as it holds at least 1.1 litres (2 pints). A wide, shallow cake makes a better-looking toadstool. Make the cake mixture (see page 16), half-fill the food can and put the remaining mixture into the pudding basin. Bake for about 30 minutes for the 'stalk' in the food can, and 40 minutes for the 'mushroom cap' in the pudding basin. Cool on a wire rack.

2 Take 350g (12oz) of the ready-to-roll icing. Colour a walnut-sized piece with brown food colouring, and the rest red. Colour 125g (4oz) green and leave the remaining 225g (8oz) white. Roll out the green icing and cut into a kidney shape as a 'grass' base. Fix to a cake board with a little water. Using the food can that the stalk was baked in as a template, cut a semi-circle from one side of the grass.

3 Reserve 50g (2oz) of the white icing and set aside; colour the rest yellow. Roll out the yellow icing into a long oblong to fit the stalk. Trim to neaten the edges. Spread buttercream thinly around the stalk cake then, holding the cake by the ends, set it at one end of the icing. Roll up the icing around the stalk and press the seam together. With a dab of buttercream, fix the stalk upright in the cut-out semi-circle in the green icing. Spread the top with buttercream.

4 Roll out the red icing to fit the mushroom cap. Set the cake flat on the worksurface and cover the upper surface thinly with buttercream. Lay the red icing over the cake and smooth in place. Trim around the base of the cake. Dust the worksurface lightly with cornflour and carefully turn the cake upside down.

5 Colour the remaining buttercream dark brown and put into a piping bag fitted with a small, fluted nozzle. Mark a circle in the centre of the base of the mushroom cap, where the stalk will fit. Pipe lines of buttercream radiating from this, to look like the 'gills' of a toadstool. Be sure to cover the sponge and red icing join. Carefully turn the cake the right way up and set on top of the stalk.

6 Roll out the reserved white icing and the brown icing. Cut the white icing into dots. Arrange on top of the toadstool, using a little buttercream to fix them. Cut the brown icing into a door and windows and fix to the stalk in the same way. Decorate the 'grass' with sugar flowers, sweets and butterflies.

Serves	A LITTLE EFFORT		NUTRITIONAL INFORMATION	
12	**Preparation Time** 1½ hours	**Cooking Time** 40 minutes, plus cooling	**Per Serving** 433 calories, 9.9g fat (of which 5.8g saturates), 87g carbohydrate, 0.3g salt	Vegetarian

Tiger Cake

butter to grease
1 x quantity of 3-egg chocolate Victoria sponge mixture
(see page 17)
chocolate and hazelnut spread for the filling
1 x quantity of frosting (see page 23)
yellow (or orange), black and red (or pink) food colourings
200g (7oz) ready-to-roll icing (sugar paste)
2 green jelly diamonds and 2 sticks of spaghetti
cornflour to dust

1 Grease and line two 18cm (7in) round sandwich tins. Make and bake the cake mixture according to the instructions on page 16. Leave on a wire rack to cool.

2 Sandwich the two layers together with the chocolate and hazelnut spread. Put the cake on a 25.5cm (10in) round cake board or a round tray.

3 Colour the frosting yellow (or orange). Using a palette knife, spread the frosting to cover the top and sides of the cake, leaving it slightly fluffed up to give a furry effect.

4 Colour 75g (3oz) icing black, 25g (1oz) pink and 25g (1oz) yellow (or orange). Leave the remaining icing white. Roll out the pink and yellow icing, and a third of the white icing. Cut three 2cm (³/₄in) rounds of pink, two 5cm (2in) rounds of yellow and two 2.5cm (1in) ovals of white.

5 Make ears by gently pulling the yellow rounds to make them rounded at one end. Dampen them with a little water in the centre and attach a pink circle to each to make inner ears. Pinch them together at the bottom to make them curve like ears. Leave to dry over a rolling pin, pink-side down, for about 30 minutes. Position on the cake, pressing gently into the frosting.

6 Position the white ovals to make the eyes. Dampen with a little water and attach the jelly diamonds for pupils. Place the remaining pink circle as a tongue. Divide the unrolled white icing in half and roll into two flattened balls. Place them above the pink tongue to form the tiger's cheeks. Break the spaghetti into 10cm (4in) lengths and insert these 'whiskers' into the side of the cheeks.

7 Roll a nut of the black icing into a nose, mark two nostrils and place on top of the two white cheeks. Dust the worksurface with cornflour and roll out the remaining black icing thinly. Using a knife, cut out a variety of curved stripes as shown and arrange on the cake. Add a strip to each jelly diamond 'eye'.

A LITTLE EFFORT		NUTRITIONAL INFORMATION		Serves
Preparation Time 1¹/₂ hours	**Cooking Time** 20–25 minutes, plus cooling	**Per Serving** 451 calories, 16g fat (of which 9g saturates), 76g carbohydrate, 0.4g salt	Vegetarian	**8**

3

Savoury Party Food

Cheese Wands

Funny Face Pizzas

Saucy Sausages

Chicken and Sausage Kebabs with Peanut Dip

Sticky Chicken Drumsticks

Cheese Scone Twists

Chicken Bites

Vegetable Samosas

Sausage Rolls

Mini Burgers

Omelette Bites

Cheese and Egg Tartlets

Crispy Spring Rolls

Mini Savoury Tarts

Mini Meatballs with Pitta

Mini BLT Rolls

Pinwheel Sandwiches

Traffic Light Puffs

Chicken Licken Pies

Cheese Wands

200g (7oz) self-raising flour, sifted, plus extra to dust

pinch of cayenne pepper

125g (4oz) unsalted butter, diced and chilled, plus extra to grease

125g (4oz) Parmesan, finely grated

2 medium eggs

1 tsp ready-made English mustard

sesame and poppy seeds to sprinkle

1 Put the flour, cayenne and butter into a food processor and pulse until the mixture resembles breadcrumbs. Alternatively, rub the butter into the flour in a large bowl by hand, until it resembles fine crumbs. Add the Parmesan and mix.

2 Crack one egg into a bowl. Separate the other egg, put the white to one side and add the egg yolk to the bowl with the whole egg. Mix in the mustard. Add to the flour mixture and mix together. Tip on to a board and knead lightly for 30 seconds, then wrap in clingfilm and chill for 30 minutes.

3 Preheat the oven to 180°C (160°C fan oven) mark 4. Grease two baking sheets. Roll out the pastry on a lightly floured surface to a 23 x 30.5cm (9 x 12in) rectangle, cut out 24 straws and carefully twist each straw twice. Put on the baking sheets.

4 Beat the reserved egg white with a fork until frothy and brush over the straws, then sprinkle with the sesame and poppy seeds. Bake for 18–20 minutes until golden. Remove from the oven and cool for 5 minutes, then transfer to a wire rack to cool completely.

Try Something Different

Roll out the pastry as directed in step 3, then cut out shapes with number or alphabet cutters. Omit the seeds and bake for 12–15 minutes until golden.

Makes 24	EASY		NUTRITIONAL INFORMATION	
	Preparation Time 10 minutes, plus chilling and cooling	**Cooking Time** 18–20 minutes	**Per Serving** 96 calories, 6.5g fat (of which 4g saturates), 6.3g carbohydrate, 0.3g salt	Vegetarian

Funny Face Pizzas

400g (14oz) strong white flour, plus extra to dust

1 tsp salt

2 tsp fast-action (easy-blend) dried yeast

2 tbsp olive oil, plus extra to grease

100ml (3½fl oz) pizza sauce or tomato pasta sauce

250g bag grated Cheddar or mozzarella cheese

a few slices of ham or salami

a few pitted olives

12 cherry tomatoes, sliced

green, red or yellow peppers, seeded and cut into strips

1 Sift the flour with the salt into a large bowl. Stir in the yeast. Make a well in the centre and pour in about 200ml (7fl oz) warm water and the oil. Mix together with a wooden spoon to form a soft dough.

2 Tip the dough on to a floured worksurface and knead for 10 minutes until smooth and elastic. Put into a lightly oiled bowl and cover with a clean teatowel. Leave to rise for 1 hour or until doubled in size.

3 Preheat the oven to 230°C (210°C fan oven) mark 8. Divide the dough into twelve pieces. Roll out each piece to the size of a saucer – about 14cm (5½in) – and arrange on lightly oiled baking sheets.

4 Spread some sauce on each pizza base, then sprinkle with cheese. Use the ham or salami, olives, cherry tomatoes and peppers to make faces on the pizzas. Bake for 5 minutes, then reduce the temperature to 200°C (180°C fan oven) mark 6 and bake for another 10–15 minutes.

Makes **12**	**EASY**		**NUTRITIONAL INFORMATION**
	Preparation Time 40 minutes, plus 1 hour rising	**Cooking Time** 20 minutes	**Per Serving** 231 calories, 9.1g fat (of which 4.9g saturates), 27.7g carbohydrate, 1g salt

Try Something Different

Use hot-dog sausages instead of skinless sausages and heat according to the packet instructions.

Saucy Sausages

4 tbsp tomato ketchup, plus extra to serve

2 tsp mild mustard

12 skinless pork sausages, about 350g (12oz) total weight

butter for spreading

12 small finger rolls

1 Preheat the grill to medium. Mix together the tomato ketchup and mustard. Coat the sausages lightly with the mixture.

2 Arrange on a foil-lined grill pan and cook under the grill, turning often, until browned and cooked through. Serve hot or cold in buttered finger rolls with extra ketchup.

EASY		NUTRITIONAL INFORMATION	Makes
Preparation Time 5 minutes	**Cooking Time** 15–20 minutes	**Per Serving** 214 calories, 11g fat (of which 3.9g saturates), 23.4g carbohydrate, 1.3g salt	**12**

Try Something Different

Serve the kebabs hot. Add the cherry tomatoes to the skewers before grilling, then serve with the dip and cooked corn on the cob cut into thick slices.

Cook's Tip

To prevent the skewers from burning, soak them in cold water for 20 minutes before assembling the kebabs.

Chicken and Sausage Kebabs with Peanut Dip

2 skinless chicken breasts, cut into bite-sized chunks

8 frankfurters, chopped

2 tbsp sunflower oil

1 medium onion, finely chopped

4 tbsp smooth peanut butter

2 tbsp tomato ketchup

16 cherry tomatoes, halved if large

ground black pepper

1 Preheat the grill to medium. Thread the chicken and frankfurters alternately on to eight wooden kebab skewers (see Cook's Tip).

2 Brush the kebabs with half the oil and cook for 15–20 minutes, turning often, until cooked through and the chicken juices run clear when pierced with the tip of a knife.

3 Meanwhile, to make the dip, heat the remaining oil in a non-stick pan. Add the onion and cook for 3–5 minutes until softened. Transfer to a blender or food processor and add the peanut butter, tomato ketchup, a little pepper and 2 tbsp water. Process until smooth.

4 Leave the kebabs to cool, add the tomatoes and serve with the dip. Remove the kebabs from the skewers if serving to very young children.

Makes 8	EASY		NUTRITIONAL INFORMATION	
	Preparation Time 15 minutes	**Cooking Time** 25 minutes, plus cooling	**Per Serving** 243 calories, 19.4g fat (of which 5.8g saturates), 3.3g carbohydrate, 1.3g salt	Dairy free

Try Something Different

Instead of drumsticks, use 450g (1lb) chicken wings and cook for 25–30 minutes.

Sticky Chicken Drumsticks

4 tbsp tomato ketchup

1 tbsp clear honey

1 tbsp mild mustard

2 tbsp dark soy sauce

1 garlic clove, crushed (optional)

8 chicken drumsticks

cherry tomatoes, halved, to serve

1　Put the ketchup, honey, mustard, soy sauce and garlic, if you like, in a large bowl. Make three deep slashes in each chicken drumstick and add to the marinade. Cover and leave overnight in the fridge.

2　Preheat the oven to 200°C (180°C fan oven) mark 6. Put the drumsticks and their marinade into a roasting tin and cook for 35 minutes until the juices run clear when pierced with the tip of a sharp knife. Eat hot or cold with cherry tomatoes.

EASY		NUTRITIONAL INFORMATION		Makes
Preparation Time 5 minutes, plus overnight marinating	**Cooking Time** 35 minutes	**Per Serving** 123 calories, 5.3g fat (of which 1.4g saturates), 3.8g carbohydrate, 1.2g salt	Dairy free	**8**

Try Something Different

If catering for older children, add a pinch of cayenne pepper to the flour in step 1 and sprinkle with 25g (1oz) Parmesan in step 4.

75g (3oz) butter, plus extra to grease

450g (1lb) self-raising flour, plus extra to dust

2 tsp baking powder

125g (4oz) mature Cheddar, finely grated

about 300ml (½ pint) milk, plus extra to glaze

salt

Cheese Scone Twists

1 Preheat the oven to 220°C (200°C fan oven) mark 7. Lightly grease two (or three) baking sheets. Sift the flour, baking powder and a pinch of salt together into a bowl, then rub in the butter. Add half the cheese and stir in enough milk to make a soft, but not sticky, dough. Knead briefly to bring together.

2 Roll out on a floured worksurface to a thickness of 1cm (½in). Cut out rounds with a 7.5cm (3in) cutter and remove the centres using a 4cm (1½in) cutter.

3 Lightly knead the trimmings, including the 4cm (1½in) rounds, and roll out again. Cut out more scone rings until all the dough is used.

4 Twist each ring to form a figure of eight and space well apart on the baking trays. Brush with milk and sprinkle with the remaining cheese. Bake for about 12 minutes until well risen and golden brown. Leave to cool on a wire rack.

	EASY		NUTRITIONAL INFORMATION	
Makes **14**	**Preparation Time** 15 minutes	**Cooking Time** 12 minutes	**Per Serving** 193 calories, 8.1g fat (of which 5.1g saturates), 25.5g carbohydrate, 0.6g salt	Vegetarian

Cook's Tip

For a vegetarian version, replace the chicken with the same amount of soya mince and complete the recipe. Cook for 15–20 minutes until golden brown.

Chicken Bites

400g (14oz) minced chicken
150g (5oz) brown breadcrumbs
100g (3½oz) mature Cheddar, grated
1 tbsp mayonnaise
1 garlic clove, crushed
1 medium egg, beaten
butter to grease
salt and ground black pepper
mayonnaise or sweet chilli sauce to serve

1 Preheat the oven to 180°C (160°C fan oven) mark 4. Put the minced chicken into a large bowl. Add two-thirds of the breadcrumbs, the Cheddar, mayonnaise and garlic. Season with salt and pepper and mix together.

2 Shape the mixture into golf-ball-sized bites. Pour the egg into a shallow dish. Put the remaining breadcrumbs on a plate. Roll each ball first in the egg, then in the breadcrumbs. Put the bites on a greased baking sheet and cook for 20–25 minutes until crisp and cooked through. Serve with mayonnaise or sweet chilli sauce.

EASY		NUTRITIONAL INFORMATION	Makes

Preparation Time
20 minutes

Cooking Time
20–25 minutes

Per Serving
106 calories, 4.3g fat (of which 1.9g saturates),
7.8g carbohydrate, 0.4g salt

15

Vegetable Samosas

1 medium potato, peeled and diced
25g (1oz) each frozen peas and sweetcorn
½ tsp mild curry paste
2 tbsp full-fat soft cheese
about 5 large sheets of filo pastry
vegetable oil to brush
poppy and sesame seeds for sprinkling
salt and ground black pepper

1 Preheat the oven to 200°C (180°C fan oven) mark 6. Cook the potato in a pan of lightly salted boiling water for 10 minutes or until just tender. Add the peas and sweetcorn and cook for another 2 minutes. Leave to drain for at least a couple of minutes.

2 Put the vegetables in a large bowl and stir in the curry paste and cheese. Season with salt and pepper to taste. Leave to cool.

3 Lay the filo pastry sheets on top of each other and cut lengthways into strips about 9cm (3½in) wide. Cover with a damp teatowel as you work to stop the strips drying out.

4 Peel away one of the strips and put a heaped teaspoonful of the filling at the end. Fold the pastry diagonally across the filling so that it makes a triangle. Keep folding along the length of the pastry. Repeat with the rest of the pastry and filling, brushing the end of the pastry with water to seal.

5 Put the samosas on a baking sheet, brush with oil and sprinkle with poppy and sesame seeds. Bake for about 15–20 minutes until golden brown. Eat warm or cold.

Cook's Tip

Leave the vegetables to drain for a few minutes so that the potatoes dry out, otherwise the samosas might be soggy.

Get Ahead

To prepare ahead Complete the recipe to the end of step 4. Put the samosas on a baking sheet, cover with clingfilm and chill for up to one day.
To use Complete the recipe.

EASY		NUTRITIONAL INFORMATION		Makes
Preparation Time 35 minutes	**Cooking Time** 15–20 minutes	**Per Serving** 76 calories, 3.1g fat (of which 0.9g saturates), 11.1g carbohydrate, 0g salt	Vegetarian	**15**

Try Something Different

For a slightly spicy version, add ½ tsp mild curry powder to the sausagemeat.
For a herby version, add 1 tsp dried sage to the sausagemeat.

Sausage Rolls

flour to dust
450g (1lb) ready-made puff pastry
450g (1lb) pork sausagemeat
a little milk
1 medium egg, beaten

1 Preheat the oven to 220°C (200°C fan oven) mark 7. On a lightly floured surface, roll out half the pastry to a 40.5 x 20.5cm (16 x 8in) rectangle. Cut lengthways into two strips. Repeat with the remaining pastry.

2 Divide the sausagemeat into four pieces, dust with flour and form into rolls the length of the pastry strips. Lay a sausagemeat roll on each pastry strip.

3 Brush the pastry edges with a little milk, fold one side of the pastry over the sausagemeat and press the two long edges firmly together with a fork to seal.

4 Brush the pastry with egg, then cut each roll into 5cm (2in) lengths. Place on baking sheets and bake for 15 minutes. Reduce the temperature to 180°C (160°C fan oven) mark 4 and cook for a further 15 minutes. Serve hot or cold.

Makes 28	EASY		NUTRITIONAL INFORMATION
	Preparation Time 25 minutes	**Cooking Time** 30 minutes	**Per Serving** 119 calories, 9.1g fat (of which 2g saturates), 7.5g carbohydrate, 0.4g salt

500g pack lean minced beef

1 small onion, finely chopped

2 tbsp vegetable stock powder

1 tbsp olive oil

12 soft mini dinner rolls

¼ iceberg lettuce, finely shredded

2 medium tomatoes, sliced

ketchup to serve

flags to decorate (optional)

Mini Burgers

1 Put the minced beef into a large bowl with the onion and stock powder and mix well. Shape the meat into 12 balls, then flatten slightly to make mini burger shapes.

2 Heat the oil in a non-stick frying pan and cook the burgers over a high heat for about 1–2 minutes on each side until well browned. Reduce the heat and continue to cook for a further 1–2 minutes until the burgers are cooked through.

3 Split open the rolls and fill with lettuce, tomato slices and a burger. Decorate with flags, if you like, and serve with ketchup.

EASY		NUTRITIONAL INFORMATION		Serves
Preparation Time 10 minutes	**Cooking Time** 6 minutes	**Per Serving** 90 calories, 5.3g fat (of which 1.9g saturates), 1.3g carbohydrate, 0.6g salt	Dairy free	**12**

Omelette Bites

8 medium eggs
1 tbsp each freshly chopped parsley and chives
15g (½oz) butter
fillings (see below)
salt and ground black pepper

1 Whisk the eggs with salt, pepper and 4 tbsp cold water. Stir in the herbs. Heat the butter in a 25.5cm (10in) non-stick frying pan. Add a small ladleful of the egg mixture and swirl it around the pan to give a thin layer. Leave for about 30 seconds to set and brown.

2 Loosen around the edges, then turn out the omelette on to a sheet of greaseproof paper.

3 Repeat with the remaining mixture to make a stack of omelettes, putting greaseproof paper between each omelette. Cover and cool.

4 Once cool, spread the omelettes with one or more of the suggested savoury fillings, then roll up and slice into 2.5cm (1in) pieces to serve.

Choose a filling

- Mix chopped cooked chicken with roughly chopped watercress sprigs and a little mayonnaise. Season to taste with salt and pepper and Dijon mustard.
- Mix small cooked and peeled prawns with garlic mayonnaise, chopped cucumber and a little grated lemon zest and lemon juice. Season to taste.
- Spread sliced salami or ham over the omelettes. Top with a little soft cheese and some shredded salad leaves.
- Mix coarsely grated carrots, fennel and celery sticks. Add a dash of natural yogurt, lemon juice and wholegrain mustard, and plenty of chopped parsley. Mix in grated Cheddar or Lancashire cheese to taste.
- Roughly chop tomatoes and radishes and roll inside the omelettes with salad leaves and a dash of lemon mayonnaise or Greek-style natural yogurt.

EASY		NUTRITIONAL INFORMATION	Makes
Preparation Time 10 minutes	**Cooking Time** 10 minutes	**Per Serving** 47 calories, 3.7g fat (of which 0.9g saturates), 0.1g carbohydrate, 0.1g salt	**40**

Get Ahead

To prepare ahead Complete the recipe to the end of step 1, cool, then store the tartlet cases in airtight containers for up to two weeks.
To use Complete the recipe.

Cheese and Egg Tartlets

12 thin slices white bread

25g (1oz) butter, melted

2 hard-boiled eggs, finely chopped

50g (2oz) Cheddar, grated

2–3 tbsp mayonnaise

mustard and cress

salt and ground black pepper

1 Preheat the oven to 180°C (160°C fan oven) mark 4. Flatten the bread slightly with a rolling pin and cut out rounds with a 7.5cm (3in) fluted cutter. Brush with melted butter and press into the holes of a bun tin. Sit another bun tin on top to keep the bread pressed down and bake for 15–20 minutes until golden brown and crisp. Cool on a wire rack.

2 Mix the hard-boiled eggs with the cheese and mayonnaise. Season with salt and pepper. Divide between the tartlet cases and sprinkle with the mustard and cress.

Makes 12	EASY		NUTRITIONAL INFORMATION	
	Preparation Time 15 minutes	**Cooking Time** 15–20 minutes	**Per Serving** 134 calories, 7.3g fat (of which 2.8g saturates), 13.4g carbohydrate, 0.5g salt	Vegetarian

Get Ahead

To prepare ahead Complete the recipe to the end of step 2, then pack into airtight containers and freeze for up to one month.
To use Thaw overnight in the fridge; complete the recipe.

Cook's Tip

You can cook the spring rolls 2–3 hours ahead, then reheat them on a foil-lined baking sheet at 200°C (180°C fan oven) mark 6 for about 10 minutes.

1 tbsp vegetable oil

1 garlic clove, crushed

1 tsp Thai seasoning

175g (6oz) minced pork

1 tbsp each fish sauce and light soy sauce

125g (4oz) carrot, grated

50g (2oz) celery, diced

50g (2oz) fresh bean sprouts

225g (8oz) filo pastry

1 egg yolk

vegetable oil for deep-frying

sweet chilli dipping sauce to serve

Crispy Spring Rolls

1 In a frying pan or wok, heat the 1 tbsp oil with the garlic and Thai seasoning and fry the pork until browned. Turn up the heat and add the fish and soy sauces, carrot and celery. Cook, stirring, for a few minutes until the liquid has evaporated. Off the heat, stir in the bean sprouts. Tip into a bowl to cool.

2 Cut the filo pastry into strips 7.5cm (3in) wide and 20.5cm (8in) long (you'll need 32 lengths). Put a heaped teaspoonful of the cooled mixture at one end of a pastry strip, fold in 1cm (½in) of pastry down both sides and roll up the filling in the pastry strip. Brush the end with egg yolk to seal it. Repeat until all the filling has been used.

3 Heat vegetable oil in a deep-fryer to 190°C (test by frying a small cube of bread; it should brown in 20 seconds). Deep-fry five or six rolls at a time for 3–4 minutes until golden brown. Drain on kitchen paper. Serve warm with a mild sweet chilli dipping sauce.

A LITTLE EFFORT		NUTRITIONAL INFORMATION		Makes
Preparation Time 30 minutes	**Cooking Time** 20 minutes	**Per Spring Roll** 75 calories, 5.3g fat (of which 0.8g saturates), 4.9g carbohydrate, 0.2g salt	Dairy free	**32**

Mini Savoury Tarts

225g (8oz) plain flour, sifted
125g (4oz) butter, plus extra to grease
2 medium eggs
225ml (8fl oz) semi-skimmed milk
2 spring onions, trimmed and chopped
100g can tuna steak in brine, drained and flaked
2 small tomatoes, chopped
25g (1oz) Cheddar, finely grated
2 slices lean cooked ham, chopped
salt

1 Put the flour and butter into a food processor with a pinch of salt. Process until the mixture resembles fine breadcrumbs. With the motor running, add just enough ice-cold water to bring the mixture together. Alternatively, rub the butter into the flour in a large bowl by hand, until the mixture resembles fine breadcrumbs, and blend in the water with a flat-bladed knife. Knead lightly until smooth, then wrap in clingfilm and chill for 30 minutes.

2 Preheat the oven to 200°C (180°C fan oven) mark 6. Roll out the pastry to a thickness of 3mm (⅛in). Grease two 12-hole bun tins. Cut out 7.5cm (3in) pastry rounds with a fluted cutter and press each round into the bun tin.

3 Beat the eggs with the milk in a jug. Put a little spring onion and some flakes of tuna in eight of the pastry cases. In another eight cases, arrange pieces of tomato and sprinkle with cheese. Divide the chopped ham among the remaining cases. Pour the egg custard mixture into the pastry cases.

4 Bake for 35 minutes, or until the filling is just set and the pastry lightly browned. Cool on a wire rack.

Try Something Different

Vary the fillings to suit the preferences and ages of the children. Chopped cooked chicken, peas, mushrooms, crisp bacon, cooked vegetables and smoked mackerel are also delicious.

Makes	EASY		NUTRITIONAL INFORMATION
24	**Preparation Time** 30 minutes, plus chilling	**Cooking Time** 35 minutes	**Per Serving** 93 calories, 5.5g fat (of which 3.3g saturates), 8.1g carbohydrate, 0.2g salt

Get Ahead

To prepare ahead Complete the recipe to the end of step 1, then put the meatballs in an airtight container and chill for up to 24 hours. Alternatively, open-freeze on a baking sheet. Once frozen, put in a freezerproof container in the freezer for up to one month.
To use Thaw overnight in the fridge, then reheat, covered with foil, in the oven for 15–20 minutes at 200°C (180°C fan oven) mark 6.

Cook's Tip

For a vegetarian version, replace the lamb with soya mince.

500g (1lb 2oz) lean minced lamb

1 small onion, very finely chopped

1 tbsp tomato purée

1 tbsp freshly chopped mint

1 tbsp sunflower oil

150g tub natural yogurt

2 tbsp hummus

juice of ½ small lemon

mini pitta breads, toasted

¼ cucumber, cut into matchsticks

salt and ground black pepper

Mini Meatballs with Pitta

1 Put the minced lamb, onion, tomato purée and mint in a bowl and season with salt and pepper. Mix everything together, then shape into 18 small balls.

2 Heat the oil in a non-stick frying pan and cook the meatballs over a medium heat for 15 minutes until golden brown and cooked through.

3 Mix together the yogurt, hummus and lemon juice, and season. Split the pitta breads and spread with the yogurt mixture, then top with cucumber and meatballs. Serve hot or cold.

EASY		NUTRITIONAL INFORMATION
Preparation Time 15 minutes	**Cooking Time** 15 minutes	**Per Serving** 272 calories, 9.8g fat (of which 3.8g saturates), 31.4g carbohydrate, 0.8g salt

Serves
9

Mini BLT Rolls

12 rashers unsmoked streaky bacon

3 tbsp mayonnaise

2 tsp grated lemon zest

12 small finger rolls

12 Little Gem lettuce leaves

12–24 cherry tomatoes, halved

1 Preheat the grill to medium and line the base of a grill pan with foil. Grill the bacon for 3–4 minutes, turning halfway through cooking, until lightly crisp at the edges. Drain on kitchen paper.

2 Put the mayonnaise in a small bowl and stir in the lemon zest. Split each roll in half and spread the mayonnaise on the bottom half. Lay a lettuce leaf on top. Cut each rasher of bacon in half and put on top of the lettuce, along with the cherry tomatoes.

3 Add the tops of the rolls and secure with a cocktail stick flag bearing the name of the guest, or the words 'Happy Birthday'.

EASY		NUTRITIONAL INFORMATION		Serves
Preparation Time 10 minutes	**Cooking Time** about 5 minutes	**Per Serving** 131 calories, 7.5g fat (of which 1.9g saturates), 12g carbohydrate, 0.8g salt	Dairy free	**12**

Pinwheel Sandwiches

6 thin slices wholemeal bread, crusts removed

6 thin slices white bread, crusts removed

1 x quantity Egg Mayonnaise (see page 27)

¹⁄₄ cucumber

125g (4oz) soft cream cheese

wafer-thin slices of ham

2 carrots, finely grated

1　Flatten the bread slightly with a rolling pin. Spread the wholemeal slices with the egg mayonnaise. Peel off long strips of cucumber with a peeler and lay across the egg. Roll up the bread gently but firmly, wrap in clingfilm and chill for a few hours.

2　Spread the white slices with the cream cheese. Lay the ham on top and spread with more cream cheese. Sprinkle the carrot over the cheese, roll up the bread gently but firmly, wrap in clingfilm and chill.

3　When ready to serve, cut each roll into five rounds. Arrange on a plate with the fillings facing upwards.

	EASY	NUTRITIONAL INFORMATION
Makes **60**	**Preparation Time** 30 minutes, plus chilling	**Per Serving** 42 calories, 2.9g fat (of which 1g saturates), 2.8g carbohydrate, 0.2g salt

Traffic Light Puffs

375g pack ready-rolled puff pastry

1 medium egg, beaten

1 yellow pepper, seeded

9 cherry tomatoes, halved

2 tbsp red or green pesto

100g (3½oz) mozzarella cheese, grated

1 small courgette, sliced into rounds

1 Preheat the oven to 200°C (180°C fan oven) mark 6. Unroll the sheet of pastry and cut into 18 rectangles, each 12.5 x 4cm (5 x 1½in). Score a line 5mm (¼in) from the edge of each rectangle to make a border. Prick with a fork all over inside the scored lines. Brush with egg and bake for 10 minutes.

2 Meanwhile, cut out circles of yellow pepper about the same size as the cherry tomato halves.

3 Take the pastry out of the oven and spread each rectangle with pesto and sprinkle with mozzarella. Top each rectangle with a courgette circle, then a piece of pepper, then a cherry tomato half. Return to the oven for another 10 minutes. Serve hot or cold.

EASY		NUTRITIONAL INFORMATION		Makes
Preparation Time 30 minutes	**Cooking Time** 20 minutes	**Per Serving** 115 calories, 8.1g fat (of which 1.2g saturates), 8.5g carbohydrate, 0.3g salt	Vegetarian	**18**

Chicken Licken Pies

200g (7oz) roasted chicken breasts, shredded
75g (3oz) cooked smoked ham, cubed
100ml (3½fl oz) double cream
50ml (2fl oz) chicken gravy
2 tbsp freshly chopped parsley
1 tsp cornflour
½ tsp English mustard
butter to grease
flour to dust
500g pack shortcrust pastry
1 egg, beaten
ground black pepper

1 Put the chicken in a large bowl with the ham. Add the cream, gravy, parsley, cornflour and mustard. Season with pepper and mix together.

2 Grease a 12-hole bun tin. Sprinkle a worksurface lightly with flour and roll out the pastry to a thickness of 3mm (⅛in). Cut out 12 large pastry discs using a 9cm (3½in) fluted cutter, then 12 small discs using a 6.5cm (2½in) fluted cutter. Line the bun tin with the large discs.

3 Using a teaspoon, fill the pastry cases with the chicken mixture. Dampen the edges of the small pastry discs on one side by brushing them with a little cold water. Gently press the small discs, damp-side down, on top of the filled pastry cases and seal the edges. Brush the tops with the beaten egg. Prick the lids with a fork to allow the steam to escape while cooking. Chill for 30 minutes. Preheat the oven to 200°C (180°C fan oven) mark 6.

4 Bake for 15–20 minutes until golden brown and piping hot. Serve hot or cold.

Cook's Tip

For a vegetarian version, replace the chicken and ham with frozen mixed vegetables and the chicken gravy with vegetable stock.

Makes	EASY		NUTRITIONAL INFORMATION
12	**Preparation Time** 20 minutes, plus chilling	**Cooking Time** 15–20 minutes	**Per Serving** 261 calories, 17.5g fat (of which 7.1g saturates), 20.4g carbohydrate, 0.7g salt

4

Sweet Party Food

Try Something Different

Chocolate Fairy Cakes: replace 2 tbsp of the flour with the same amount of cocoa powder.

Stir 50g (2oz) chocolate drops, sultanas or chopped dried apricots into the mixture at the end of step 1. Complete the recipe.

Fairy Cakes

125g (4oz) self-raising flour, sifted
1 tsp baking powder
125g (4oz) caster sugar
125g (4oz) butter, very soft
2 medium eggs
1 tbsp milk
225g (8oz) icing sugar, sifted
assorted food colourings (optional)
sweets, sprinkles or coloured sugar to decorate

1 Preheat the oven to 200°C (180°C fan oven) mark 6. Put paper cases into 18 of the holes in two bun tins. Put the flour, baking powder, sugar, butter, eggs and milk in a mixing bowl and beat with an electric hand whisk for 2 minutes until the mixture is pale and very soft.

2 Half-fill each paper case with the mixture. Bake for 10–15 minutes until golden brown. Transfer to a wire rack to cool.

3 Put the icing sugar in a bowl and gradually blend in 2–3 tbsp warm water until the icing is fairly stiff, but spreadable. Add a couple of drops of food colouring, if you like. When the cakes are cold, spread the tops with the icing and decorate.

Makes **18**	EASY		NUTRITIONAL INFORMATION	
	Preparation Time 20 minutes	**Cooking Time** 10–15 minutes, plus cooling	**Per Serving** 160 calories, 6.4g fat (of which 3.9g saturates), 25.8g carbohydrate, 0.2g salt	Vegetarian

125g (4oz) butter, very soft

175g (6oz) plain white flour, sifted, plus extra to dust

50g (2oz) caster sugar

1/2 tsp vanilla extract

milk

18 coloured boiled sweets

1 x quantity glacé icing (see page 22)

edible coloured balls to decorate

Jewel Biscuits

1 Line three baking sheets with non-stick baking parchment. Put the butter, flour, sugar and vanilla extract in a bowl and bring together with a fork or wooden spoon to form a dough – add a drop of milk if the mixture looks too dry. Turn out on to a floured worksurface and knead briefly to bring the dough together. Wrap in clingfilm and chill for 30 minutes.

2 Preheat the oven to 180°C (160°C fan oven) mark 4. Roll out the dough until it is about 3mm (1/8in) thick (sprinkle the surface of the dough with flour if it starts to stick). Using novelty biscuit cutters, cut out different shapes and arrange on the baking sheets. Using small cutters, cut a shape from the middle of each biscuit and put a sweet in each hole.

3 Bake for about 10–15 minutes until the biscuits are pale golden brown and the sweets have melted. Leave to set for a minute, then transfer to a wire rack to cool. When the biscuits are cold, decorate with glacé icing and edible balls.

A LITTLE EFFORT		NUTRITIONAL INFORMATION		Makes
Preparation Time	**Cooking Time**	**Per Serving**		**18**
30 minutes, plus chilling	10–15 minutes, plus cooling	164 calories, 5.8g fat (of which 3.8g saturates), 28.8g carbohydrate, 0.1g salt	Vegetarian	

Cook's Tips

These biscuits are gluten-free; if this is not a concern you can use plain flour and baking powder.
Store un-iced biscuits in an airtight container for up to one week.

Gluten-free Spiced Star Biscuits

2 tbsp clear honey

25g (1oz) unsalted butter, plus extra to grease

50g (2oz) light muscovado sugar

finely grated zest of ½ lemon

finely grated zest of ½ orange

225g (8oz) gluten-free flour (see Cook's Tips), plus extra to dust

1 tsp wheat-free baking powder (see Cook's Tips)

1 tsp ground cinnamon

1 tsp ground ginger

½ tsp freshly grated nutmeg

pinch of ground cloves

pinch of salt

1 tbsp finely chopped candied peel

50g (2oz) ground almonds

1 large egg, beaten

2–3 tbsp milk

glacé icing (see page 22) (optional)

edible silver balls to decorate (optional)

1 Put the honey, butter, sugar and citrus zests into a small pan and stir over a low heat until the butter has melted and the ingredients are well combined.

2 Sift the flour, baking powder, spices and salt together in a bowl, then add the candied peel and ground almonds. Add the melted mixture, beaten egg and milk and mix until the dough comes together, adding a little extra milk if the dough feels crumbly. Knead the dough briefly until smooth, then wrap in clingfilm and chill for at least 4 hours or overnight.

3 Preheat the oven to 180°C (160°C fan oven) mark 4. Roll out the dough on a lightly floured surface to a thickness of 5mm (¼in). Stamp out stars using a 5cm (2in) cutter and put on several greased baking sheets.

4 Bake for 15–20 minutes until just beginning to brown at the edges. Transfer the biscuits to a wire rack to cool. Decorate the biscuits with icing and silver balls before serving, if you like.

	EASY		NUTRITIONAL INFORMATION	
Makes **35**	**Preparation Time** 15 minutes, plus chilling	**Cooking Time** 15–20 minutes, plus cooling	**Per Serving** 34 calories, 2g fat (of which 0.5g saturates), 4g carbohydrate, 0g salt	Vegetarian Gluten free

Cook's Tip

To save time, look out for coloured ready-to-roll icings, which are available in major supermarkets or specialist cake decorating shops.

Dinosaur Biscuits

25g (1oz) plain white flour, sifted, plus extra to dust
175g (6oz) plain wholemeal flour, sifted
1 tsp baking powder
75g (3oz) cold butter, diced
25g (1oz) caster sugar
25g (1oz) porridge oats
about 5 tbsp milk
450g (1lb) white ready-to-roll icing (sugar paste)
assorted food colourings
icing sugar to dust
assorted writing icings

1 Line three baking sheets with non-stick baking parchment. Put both flours and the baking powder into a large bowl and rub in the butter with your fingertips until the mixture resembles breadcrumbs. Alternatively, you can do this in a food processor. Stir in the caster sugar and oats.

2 Gradually add the milk and, using a flat-bladed knife, bring the mixture together until it forms a soft, but not too sticky dough. Tip on to a floured worksurface and knead briefly until smooth. Wrap in clingfilm and chill for 30 minutes.

3 Preheat the oven to 200°C (180°C fan oven) mark 6. Roll out the dough on a floured worksurface to a thickness of 3mm (⅛in). Cut out dinosaur shapes using biscuit cutters. Put the biscuits on the baking sheets and bake for 10–15 minutes until a pale golden colour. Cool on wire racks.

4 When the biscuits are cold, divide the icing into three or four pieces. Colour each piece with a few drops of food colouring and knead until the colour is evenly distributed. Dust the worksurface and a rolling pin with icing sugar and roll out the icing. Use the biscuit cutters to cut out dinosaur shapes. Brush the underside of the icing shapes with a little water and stick to the biscuits. Use the writing icing to draw on scales, eyes and smiles.

A LITTLE EFFORT		NUTRITIONAL INFORMATION		Makes
Preparation Time	**Cooking Time**	**Per Serving**		**16**
45 minutes, plus chilling	10–15 minutes, plus cooling	187 calories, 4.3g fat (of which 2.6g saturates), 36.9g carbohydrate, 0.1g salt	Vegetarian	

Gingerbread Footballers

125g (4oz) cold butter, diced, plus extra to grease

350g (12oz) plain flour, plus extra to dust

1 tsp bicarbonate of soda

2 tsp ground ginger

175g (6oz) soft light brown sugar

4 tbsp golden syrup

1 medium egg, beaten

assorted writing icings

star and football decorations (optional)

1 Lightly grease three baking sheets with butter. Sift the flour, bicarbonate of soda and ginger into a mixing bowl. Rub in the butter until the mixture resembles fine breadcrumbs, then stir in the sugar. Alternatively, you can do this in a food processor. Beat the golden syrup with the egg, then stir into the flour mixture and mix to make a dough. Knead until smooth, then divide in half and wrap in clingfilm. Chill for 30 minutes.

2 Preheat the oven to 190°C (170°C fan oven) mark 5. Roll out the dough, one half at a time, on a floured surface until about 5mm (¼in) thick. Using a gingerbread man cutter, cut out shapes. Repeat with the second half of the dough. Re-roll the trimmings until all of the dough has been used. Put the gingerbread men on the baking sheets.

3 Bake for 12–15 minutes until golden brown. Leave on the baking sheets to cool slightly, then transfer to wire racks.

4 When the gingerbread has cooled completely, decorate the footballers. Using black writing icing, give each man a pair of eyes and a dot for a nose. Use red icing for a mouth, and black or yellow icing for hair. Choosing the colour(s) of your child's favourite football strip, draw an outline around the edge of the gingerbread to represent a shirt and shorts, then fill in the shirt with stripes if you like. Use contrasting icing to write a number on the front of each shirt. Decorate the shorts with stars, if you like, and attach footballs with a dot of writing icing. Leave to set. Remember to remove non-edible decorations before eating.

Makes 20	EASY		NUTRITIONAL INFORMATION	
	Preparation Time 5 minutes, plus chilling	**Cooking Time** 12–15 minutes, plus cooling	**Per Serving** 157 calories, 5.7g fat (of which 3.5g saturates), 25.9g carbohydrate, 0.2g salt	Vegetarian

Mini Toffee Apples

600g (1lb 5oz) granulated sugar

10 small Cox's apples

10 bamboo skewers or lolly sticks

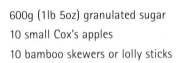

1 Line a baking sheet with non-stick baking parchment. Gently heat the sugar with 300ml (½ pint) water in a heavy-based pan until the sugar dissolves.

2 Meanwhile, spear each apple with a bamboo skewer or lolly stick. Make sure the sugar has dissolved completely (otherwise it will crystallise), then turn up the heat and boil until it turns a caramel colour. Take the pan off the heat and immediately dip the pan in cold water to stop the caramel cooking further.

3 Quickly dip each apple into the caramel to coat, then put on the baking parchment to cool. Serve within 2–3 hours, before the caramel starts to soften.

Makes 10	A LITTLE EFFORT		NUTRITIONAL INFORMATION	
	Preparation Time 10 minutes	**Cooking Time** 15 minutes	**Per Serving** 258 calories, 0.1g fat (of which 0g saturates), 68g carbohydrate, 0g salt	Vegetarian Gluten free • Dairy free

Cook's Tip

Bananas will go black if frozen for any length of time, so do not make these lollies any earlier than the evening before serving.

Jolly Lollies

450g (1lb) milk or plain chocolate, broken into pieces
10 large bananas, peeled
20 lolly sticks

For the decoration
hundreds and thousands
toasted desiccated coconut
Smarties or sugar flowers

1 Line two baking sheets with non-stick baking parchment. Put the chocolate in a heatproof bowl set over a pan of gently simmering water. Leave to melt, stirring once or twice.

2 Cut each banana in half widthways. Push a lolly stick into each banana half, then dip in the chocolate. Use a pastry brush to brush the chocolate over the banana; it should be completely coated, including the cut end. Put on the lined baking sheets. Repeat until all the bananas are covered.

3 While the chocolate is still soft, sprinkle the bananas with hundreds and thousands, desiccated coconut, Smarties or sugar flowers.

4 Once the chocolate has set, open-freeze the lollies on the baking sheets, then transfer to freezerproof containers, interleaved with greaseproof paper (see Cook's Tip). To serve, remove from the freezer about 10–15 minutes before eating.

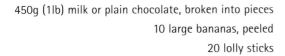

EASY	NUTRITIONAL INFORMATION		Makes
Preparation Time 25 minutes, plus freezing	**Per Serving** 175 calories, 6.8g fat (of which 3.9g saturates), 28.5g carbohydrate, 0g salt	Vegetarian Gluten free	**20**

Cook's Tip

The meringues will keep for several weeks in an airtight container.

Meringue Bones

2 medium egg whites, at room temperature

125g (4oz) caster sugar

cocoa powder to dust

1 Preheat the oven to 140°C (120°C fan oven) mark 1. Line two or three baking sheets with non-stick baking parchment. Whisk the egg whites in a large clean bowl. Add the sugar, one teaspoonful at a time, whisking until very stiff between each addition. The meringue should be very thick and glossy.

2 Spoon the meringue into a piping bag fitted with a 1cm (½in) plain nozzle. Pipe a line of meringue on a baking sheet, about 8cm (3¼in) long. At each end, pipe two small blobs to form the nubs of the bones. Continue until all the mixture has been used.

3 Bake for about 1½ hours or until hard and dry. Remove from the baking parchment and cool on a wire rack. Pile the meringues on a plate and dust lightly with cocoa powder.

Makes 16	EASY		NUTRITIONAL INFORMATION	
	Preparation Time 25 minutes	**Cooking Time** 1¼ hours	**Per Serving** 32 calories, 0g fat (of which 00g saturates), 8.2g carbohydrate, 00g salt	Vegetarian Gluten free • Dairy free

50g (2oz) very soft butter

50g (2oz) caster sugar

1 medium egg, beaten

50g (2oz) self-raising flour

¼ tsp baking powder

1 ripe banana, peeled and mashed

125g (4oz) icing sugar, sifted

about 1 tbsp orange juice

red glacé cherries or round red jelly sweets to decorate

Red Nose Buns

1 Preheat the oven to 190°C (170°C fan oven) mark 5. Put the butter, caster sugar, egg, flour and baking powder in a food processor and process until smooth and well mixed. Add the banana and process for 1 minute.

2 Arrange about 36 petits fours cases on baking sheets. Put a teaspoonful of the mixture into each case. Bake for about 12–15 minutes until golden. Transfer to a wire rack to cool.

3 When the buns are cold, make glacé icing by mixing the icing sugar with the orange juice until smooth and just thick enough to coat the back of a spoon. Top each bun with a small blob of icing and stick half a cherry or a sweet on each one. Leave to set.

EASY		NUTRITIONAL INFORMATION		Makes
Preparation Time 20 minutes	**Cooking Time** 12–15 minutes, plus cooling	**Per Serving** 39 calories, 1.3g fat (of which 0.8g saturates), 6.8g carbohydrate, 0g salt	Vegetarian	**36**

125g (4oz) butter, very soft

125g (4oz) caster sugar

grated zest of 1 lemon

2 medium eggs, beaten

125g (4oz) self-raising flour, sifted

For the decoration

175g (6oz) icing sugar

black and assorted writing icings

jelly diamonds and Smarties

black liquorice laces, cut into short lengths

Kitten Cakes

1 Preheat the oven to 190°C (170°C fan oven) mark 5. Put paper cases in a 12-hole bun tin.

2 Beat the butter, caster sugar and lemon zest together with an electric hand whisk until pale and fluffy. Add the eggs, a little at a time, beating well after each addition. Fold in the flour. Divide the mixture between the paper cases. Bake for about 20 minutes until golden and risen. Cool on a wire rack.

3 Sift the icing sugar into a bowl. Stir in 1–2 tbsp warm water, a few drops at a time, until you have a smooth, spreadable icing. Slice the tops off the cooled buns to make them level, if necessary. Cover the top of each cake with icing.

4 Decorate the buns to make kittens' faces. Use black writing icing for the eyes, halve the jelly diamonds for the ears, press a Smartie in the centre for a nose, and use black writing icing to draw on a mouth. Use different coloured writing icing for the pupils and markings. Stick on liquorice whiskers.

EASY		NUTRITIONAL INFORMATION	
Makes **12**	**Preparation Time** 25 minutes	**Cooking Time** 20 minutes, plus cooling	**Per Serving** 223 calories, 9.6g fat (of which 5.9g saturates), 34.2g carbohydrate, 0.2g salt	Vegetarian

Cherry Chocolate Chip Cookies

75g (3oz) unsalted butter, softened, plus extra to grease

25g (1oz) caster sugar

50g (2oz) light muscovado sugar

a few drops vanilla extract

1 large egg, lightly beaten

175g (6oz) self-raising flour, sifted

finely grated zest of 1 orange

125g (4oz) white chocolate, broken into pieces

125g (4oz) glacé cherries, roughly chopped

1 Preheat the oven to 180°C (160°C fan oven) mark 4 and grease several baking sheets. Using an electric hand whisk, beat together the butter, caster sugar, muscovado sugar and vanilla extract in a large bowl until well combined. Beat in the egg.

2 With a large metal spoon, lightly fold in the flour, orange zest, chocolate and glacé cherries. Put heaped teaspoonfuls of the mixture, spaced well apart, on the prepared baking sheets. Press lightly with the back of a spoon and bake for 10–12 minutes. The biscuits should be soft under a crisp crust. Leave to cool on a wire rack.

EASY		NUTRITIONAL INFORMATION		Makes
Preparation Time 20 minutes	**Cooking Time** 10–12 minutes, plus cooling	**Per Serving** 104 calories, 4.5g fat (of which 2.7g saturates), 15.4g carbohydrate, 0.1g salt	Vegetarian	**24**

Try Something Different

For a nut-free topping, make a simple glacé icing. Sift 225g (8oz) icing sugar into a bowl and mix in 2–3 tbsp orange juice to form a smooth, spreadable icing.

Wholemeal Banana Muffins

50ml (2fl oz) sunflower oil, plus extra to grease

50g (2oz) raisins

grated zest and juice of 1 orange

125g (4oz) wholemeal flour

25g (1oz) wheatgerm

3 tbsp golden caster sugar

2 tsp baking powder

pinch of salt

1 large egg, beaten

50ml (2fl oz) full-fat milk

2 medium-sized ripe bananas, about 225g (8oz) when peeled, mashed roughly

For the topping

5 tbsp orange marmalade

50g (2oz) banana chips, roughly chopped

50g (2oz) walnuts, roughly chopped

1 Put the raisins in a bowl, pour in the orange juice and leave to soak for 1 hour.

2 Preheat the oven to 200°C (180°C fan oven) mark 6. Put the orange zest in a bowl with the flour, wheatgerm, sugar, baking powder and salt and mix together. Make a well in the centre.

3 In a separate bowl, mix the egg, milk and oil, then pour into the flour mixture and stir until just blended. Drain the raisins, reserving 1 tbsp juice, and stir into the mixture with the bananas. Don't over-mix.

4 Fill each muffin case two-thirds full. Bake for 15–20 minutes until a skewer inserted into the centre comes out clean. Remove from the oven and transfer the muffins to a wire rack to cool slightly.

5 For the topping, gently heat the marmalade with the reserved orange juice until melted. Simmer for 1 minute, then add the banana chips and walnuts and spoon on top of the muffins. Serve while still warm.

Makes **24**	**EASY**		**NUTRITIONAL INFORMATION**
	Preparation Time 5 minutes	Cooking Time 20 minutes	**Per Serving** 61 calories, 2g fat (of which 0.3g saturates), 9.8g carbohydrate, 0.1g salt

butter to grease

125g (4oz) milk chocolate

9 ready-to-eat prunes

200g (7oz) light muscovado sugar

3 large egg whites

1 tsp vanilla extract

75g (3oz) plain flour, sifted

50g (2oz) white chocolate, chopped

icing sugar to dust

Chocolate Fudge Brownies

1 Preheat the oven to 180°C (160°C fan oven) mark 4. Grease and baseline a 15cm (6in) square shallow cake tin. Melt the milk chocolate in a heatproof bowl over a pan of gently simmering water. Remove from the heat and leave to cool slightly.

2 Put the prunes in a food processor or blender with 100ml (3½fl oz) water and whiz for 2–3 minutes to make a purée. Add the muscovado sugar and whiz briefly to mix.

3 In a clean, grease-free bowl, whisk the egg whites until they form soft peaks.

4 Add the vanilla extract, prune mixture, flour, white chocolate and egg whites to the bowl of melted chocolate. Fold everything together gently. Pour the mixture into the prepared tin and bake for 1 hour or until firm to the touch.

5 Leave to cool in the tin. Turn out, dust with icing sugar and cut into 12 squares.

EASY		NUTRITIONAL INFORMATION		Serves
Preparation Time 20 minutes	**Cooking Time** 1 hour, plus cooling	**Per Brownie** 174 calories, 5g fat (of which 3g saturates), 33g carbohydrate, 0.1g salt	Vegetarian	**4**

Cook's Tip

Colour the buttercream with pink or green food colouring if you like, to match the theme of the party..

Chocolate Butterfly Cakes

125g (4oz) butter, very soft
125g (4oz) caster sugar
2 medium eggs, lightly beaten individually
125g (4oz) plain flour
25g (1oz) cocoa
½ tsp baking powder
1 tbsp milk
1 x quantity of buttercream icing (see page 22)

1 Preheat the oven to 190°C (170°C fan oven) mark 5. Put 18 paper cake cases into two bun trays. With an electric hand whisk, beat the butter and sugar together until soft and fluffy and lighter in colour. Beat in the eggs thoroughly, one at a time.

2 Sift the flour, cocoa and baking powder into the bowl and fold in gently until well mixed. Fold in the milk to give a soft, dropping consistency.

3 Divide the mixture between the cases and bake for 15–20 minutes until firm. Cool on a wire rack.

4 Slice off the top of each cake and cut the slice in half. Spread buttercream on each cake with a palette knife. Put the 'butterfly wings' on top, with their curved sides facing away from each other.

Makes	EASY		NUTRITIONAL INFORMATION	
18	**Preparation Time** 25 minutes	**Cooking Time** 15–20 minutes, plus cooling	**Per Serving** 170 calories, 7g fat (of which 4.2g saturates), 26g carbohydrate, 0.2g salt	Vegetarian

Try Something Different

Replace the raisins with 50g (2oz) chopped toasted hazelnuts.

Chocolate Crispies

400g (14oz) Mars Bars, sliced

2 tbsp golden syrup

15g (½oz) butter

12 glacé cherries, diced

50g (2oz) raisins

50g (2oz) Rice Krispies

1 Put the Mars Bars, syrup and butter in a pan and heat gently until the Mars Bars have melted.

2 Add the cherries, raisins and Rice Krispies and mix together quickly. Spoon into a 25.5 x 15cm (10 x 6in) non-stick tin and level the surface; alternatively, use a 20.5cm (8in) square tin. Leave to set.

3 Turn the mixture out on to a board and cut into small squares.

EASY	NUTRITIONAL INFORMATION	Makes
Preparation Time 15 minutes, plus cooling	**Per Serving** 61 calories, 2.2g fat (of which 1.2g saturates), 10.2g carbohydrate, 0.1g salt Vegetarian	**40**

Try Something Different

Thread the fruit (when the chocolate has set) on to skewers to make fruity kebabs.

Chocolate-dipped Fruit

350g (12oz) strawberries

125g (4oz) blueberries

225g (8oz) seedless red and green grapes

75g (3oz) milk chocolate, broken into pieces

75g (3oz) white chocolate, broken into pieces

1 Wash the fruit and pat dry thoroughly on kitchen paper. Don't remove the stems from the strawberries. Line a baking sheet with non-stick baking parchment.

2 Melt the milk chocolate in a heatproof bowl set over a pan of gently simmering water. Stir a couple of times until smooth, then leave to cool until thickened to a coating consistency.

3 Partially dip half the fruits in the milk chocolate to half-coat, allowing the excess chocolate to drip back into the bowl. Use a cocktail stick to dip the blueberries. Put on the lined baking sheet. Melt the white chocolate in the same way and repeat with the remaining fruit. Leave in a cool place until set.

Serves 12	EASY	NUTRITIONAL INFORMATION	
	Preparation Time 20 minutes, plus setting	**Per Serving** 91 calories, 3.9g fat (of which 2.3g saturates), 13.5g carbohydrate, 0g salt	Vegetarian Gluten free

Cook's Tip

If you don't have a sugar thermometer, drop 1 tsp of the syrup into a bowl of cold water. If it forms a soft ball when squeezed between your finger and thumb, the syrup is at the correct temperature.

Coconut Ice

oil or butter to grease
450g (1lb) granulated sugar
150ml (¼ pint) milk
150g (5oz) desiccated coconut
few drops of red food colouring

1 Grease a 20.5 x 15cm (8 x 6in) square tin. Put the sugar and milk in a heavy-based pan and heat gently until the sugar has dissolved. Bring to the boil and boil gently for about 10 minutes, or until a temperature of 116°C (240°F) (soft ball stage) is reached on a sugar thermometer (see Cook's Tip). Plunge the base of the pan into a bowl of cold water to stop the mixture cooking further.

2 Stir in the coconut. Pour half the mixture quickly into the tin. Stir a few drops of food colouring into the other half of the mixture and pour quickly over the first layer. Leave until half-set, then mark into squares. Cut or break into squares when cold.

EASY		NUTRITIONAL INFORMATION		Makes
Preparation Time 15 minutes	**Cooking Time** 10 minutes	**Per Serving** 65 calories, 2.3g fat (of which 1.9g saturates), 11.6g carbohydrate, 0g salt	Vegetarian Gluten free	**42** pieces

Try Something Different

Instead of walnuts, use toasted hazelnuts or almonds. **For a nut-free version,** replace the walnuts with 50g (2oz) raisins.

No-cook Nutty Chocolate Fudge

125g (4oz) butter, plus extra to grease
225g (8oz) plain chocolate, broken into pieces
1 medium egg, beaten
450g (1lb) caster sugar
2 tbsp condensed milk
1 tsp vanilla extract
50g (2oz) walnuts, finely chopped

1 Grease an 18cm (7in) square tin. Melt the chocolate and butter in a heatproof bowl set over a pan of gently simmering water.

2 Mix together the egg, sugar, condensed milk and vanilla, then add the chocolate mixture. Stir in the nuts, then turn the mixture into the greased tin. Chill in the fridge overnight. Cut into squares when set.

Makes
49
pieces

EASY

Preparation Time
20 minutes, plus overnight chilling

NUTRITIONAL INFORMATION

Per Serving
90 calories, 4.3g fat (of which 2.3g saturates),
12.9g carbohydrate, 0.1g salt

Vegetarian
Gluten free

Cook's Tips

Use different food colourings to fit the theme of
your party – pink for princesses, purple or black for witches
and wizards.
The popcorn will keep for up to two days in an airtight
container.

Monster Popcorn

2 tbsp sunflower oil

125g (4oz) popping corn

450g (1lb) caster sugar

$\frac{1}{2}$ tsp green food colouring

1 Line a baking sheet with non-stick baking parchment.
Heat the oil in a large, heavy-based pan. Add the
corn, cover and cook over a high heat, shaking
occasionally, until the popping stops. Tip into a
large bowl.

2 Put the sugar and food colouring in a wide sauté pan,
along with 250ml (9fl oz) cold water. Heat gently
until the sugar has dissolved, then bring to the boil.
Without stirring, boil the mixture for 10–15 minutes
until a teaspoonful of the syrup hardens into a strand
when dropped into a bowl of cold water.

3 Take the pan off the heat and quickly stir in the
popcorn, stirring well to coat. Tip on to the lined
baking sheet and leave to cool.

EASY		NUTRITIONAL INFORMATION		Serves
Preparation Time 10 minutes	**Cooking Time** about 20 minutes	**Per Serving** 314 calories, 6.7g fat (of which 0.7g saturates), 66.4g carbohydrate, 0g salt	Vegetarian Gluten free • Dairy free	**8**

Cook's Tips

Don't worry if your baking tin is not the exact size; use one of similar dimensions.
Store the flapjack squares in an airtight container for up to one week.

Try Something Different

Instead of mixed dried fruit, use chopped dried apricots.

Fruit and Nut Flapjack Bites

250g (9oz) unsalted butter, cut into pieces, plus extra to grease

250g (9oz) caster sugar

175g (6oz) golden syrup

425g (15oz) rolled oats

125g (4oz) mixed dried fruit, including glacé cherries

75g (3oz) chopped nuts, toasted

1 Preheat the oven to 180°C (160°C fan oven) mark 4. Grease a shallow 28 x 20.5cm (11 x 8in) baking tin.

2 Put the butter, sugar and syrup in a large, heavy-based pan. Stir over a moderate heat until the butter has melted. Remove from the heat and stir in the oats, dried fruit and nuts.

3 Turn into the prepared tin and level the surface. Bake for 25–30 minutes until deep golden around the edges; the mixture will still be very soft in the middle. Leave in the tin until almost cold. Remove from the tin and cut into squares. Store in an airtight tin. It will keep for up to a week.

	EASY		**NUTRITIONAL INFORMATION**	
Makes **36**	**Preparation Time** 10 minutes	**Cooking Time** 25–30 minutes, plus cooling	**Per Serving** 162 calories, 7.9g fat (of which 3.8g saturates), 22.2g carbohydrate, 0.2g salt	Vegetarian

Try Something Different

Make traffic light jellies using red, yellow and green smoothies or juices. Make up one batch at a time and leave to set in the fridge for 2 hours before adding the next layer.

Sunset Jellies

750ml bottle mango and passion fruit smoothie

3 sachets powdered gelatine – or enough to set 1.4 litres (2½ pints) liquid according to the packet instructions

750ml bottle raspberry juice (or orange and raspberry or apple and raspberry)

1 Pour the smoothie into a pan and sprinkle half the gelatine over it. Heat gently for 5 minutes until hot but not boiling, stirring constantly to dissolve the gelatine.

2 Pour the mixture into a large jug, then divide among 12 x 125ml (4fl oz) tumblers or bowls. Cool for 15 minutes, then chill for 2 hours until set.

3 Prepare the raspberry juice in the same way as in step 1. Cool for 15 minutes, transfer to a jug and pour on top of the set jellies. Return to the fridge to set overnight.

EASY	NUTRITIONAL INFORMATION		Serves
Preparation Time 20 minutes, plus chilling and overnight setting	**Per Serving** 77 calories, 0.2g fat (of which 0.1g saturates), 16.1g carbohydrate, 0g salt	Gluten free Dairy free	**12**

5

Drinks

Witches' Brew

blue, purple or black food colouring powder
125g (4oz) granulated sugar
1 medium egg white
2 bottles of sparkling mineral water
8 tbsp blackcurrant cordial
2 tsp lemon juice
a couple of handfuls of frozen fruits of the forest

1 Mix together a little of the food colouring with the sugar until you have the depth of colour you need. Very lightly whisk the egg until just frothy. Dip the rim of each glass into the egg white, then into the sugar to form a frosted coating.

2 Pour the mineral water into a large glass jug. Add the cordial and lemon juice and stir. Put a few of the frozen berries into the bottom of each glass and top up with brew.

Serves	EASY	NUTRITIONAL INFORMATION	
12	**Preparation Time** 5 minutes	**Per Serving** 70 calories, 0g fat (of which 0g saturates), 18.1g carbohydrate, 0g salt	Vegetarian

Mud and Worm Juice

500ml (18fl oz) chocolate ice cream

jelly snake and bug sweets, plus extra to decorate

600ml (1 pint) full-fat chocolate milk

flake bars, crumbled

1 Put a scoop of ice cream in the bottom of eight tall tumblers. Drop in the jelly snakes and bugs and another scoop of ice cream.

2 Pour the milk over the ice cream. Sprinkle with crumbled flake bars and extra creepy crawlies.

EASY	NUTRITIONAL INFORMATION		Serves
Preparation Time 10 minutes	**Per Serving** 265 calories, 16.2g fat (of which 9.7g saturates), 25.3g carbohydrate, 0.2g salt	Vegetarian Gluten free	**8**

Try Something Different

Strawberry and Pineapple Smoothie: put 550g (1¼lb) strawberries, 600ml (1 pint) unsweetened pineapple juice and 450g (1lb) low-fat strawberry yogurt into a blender or food processor and blend for 1 minute or until smooth. Chill and pour into eight glasses.

Berry Smoothie

2 large bananas, about 450g (1lb), peeled and roughly chopped

150g (5oz) natural yogurt

500g bag frozen summer fruits

1 Put the bananas, yogurt and 150ml (¼ pint) water into a food processor or blender and process until smooth. Add the frozen berries and blend to a purée.

2 Sieve the mixture, using the back of a ladle to press it through. Chill and pour into glasses.

Serves 8	EASY	NUTRITIONAL INFORMATION	
	Preparation Time 10 minutes	**Per Serving** 80 calories, 0.4g fat (of which 0.2g saturates), 18.1g carbohydrate, 0g salt	Vegetarian Gluten free

Jungle Juice

12 kiwi fruit, plus extra to garnish

3 handfuls of ice cubes

750ml strawberry and kiwi sparkling water or apple juice

1 Peel the kiwi fruit, slice in half and remove the cores if hard. Put into a blender or food processor and add the ice cubes and sparkling water or juice. Process until just slushy. Pour into tumblers and garnish with kiwi slices.

EASY	NUTRITIONAL INFORMATION		Serves
Preparation Time 10 minutes	**Per Serving** 53 calories, 0.4g fat (of which 0g saturates), 12.6g carbohydrate, 0g salt	Vegetarian Gluten free • Dairy free	**12**

The Rocky Road Shake

8 small bananas

2.4 litres (4¼ pints) full-fat milk

icing sugar to taste

ice cubes

8 tbsp chocolate sauce

8 scoops vanilla ice cream

mini marshmallows

8 scoops chocolate ice cream

4 flake bars, halved, to decorate

1 Put the bananas in a blender or food processor with a little of the milk and blend until smooth. Add the rest of the milk, with a little icing sugar and a handful of ice cubes, and blend again. Taste for sweetness and add more icing sugar if necessary.

2 Divide the chocolate sauce between eight tall tumblers. Top with a scoop of vanilla ice cream, followed by some marshmallows and a scoop of chocolate ice cream. Pour in the banana milkshake. Sprinkle with more marshmallows and decorate with a piece of chocolate flake.

Serves 8	EASY	NUTRITIONAL INFORMATION	
	Preparation Time 10 minutes	**Per Serving** 479 calories, 23.3g fat (of which 14g saturates), 56.9g carbohydrate, 0.6g salt	Vegetarian

Apple and Ginger Fizz

1 litre (1³/₄ pints) apple juice
1 litre (1³/₄ pints) ginger ale
2 apples, peeled, sliced and cut into stars

1 Put the apple juice and ginger ale in a large jug or bowl, add the apple shapes, reserving 12 for decoration. Stir to mix, then pour into glasses. Decorate with apple shapes on cocktail sticks.

EASY	NUTRITIONAL INFORMATION		Serves
Preparation Time 10 minutes	**Per Serving** 50 calories, 0.1g fat (of which 0g saturates), 13g carbohydrate, 0g salt	Vegetarian Gluten free • Dairy free	**12**

Fairy Cocktail

225g (8oz) fresh or frozen raspberries

150g (5oz) Greek yogurt

1 litre (1¾ pints) full-fat milk

icing sugar to taste

crushed ice

hundreds and thousands or pink sprinkles to decorate

1 medium egg white

1 Put the raspberries in a blender or food processor and blend until smooth. Sieve into a bowl to remove the pips. Return the purée to the blender.

2 Add the yogurt and 150ml (¼ pint) milk and blend until smooth.

3 Add the remaining milk and a little icing sugar and blend again. Taste for sweetness and add more icing sugar if necessary. Pour into a jug with crushed ice.

4 Put the hundreds and thousands or pink sprinkles into a bowl. Lightly whisk the egg white in another bowl. Dip the rim of each glass into the egg white, then into the sprinkles. Carefully pour in the cocktails and decorate with magic wands.

Serves 8	EASY	NUTRITIONAL INFORMATION	
	Preparation Time 10 minutes	**Per Serving** 113 calories, 6.9g fat (of which 4g saturates), 7.7g carbohydrate, 0.2g salt	Vegetarian Gluten free

Mango Banana Smoothie

2 extra large ripe mangoes, peeled and chopped

3 bananas, peeled and chopped

600ml (1 pint) full-fat milk

600ml (1 pint) unsweetened orange juice

150g (5oz) Greek yogurt

icing sugar to taste

1 Put all the ingredients except the icing sugar into a blender or food processor and blend for 1 minute or until smooth. Taste for sweetness and add a little icing sugar if necessary. Blend briefly.

2 Chill for up to 2 hours until required, then pour into eight glasses and serve.

EASY	NUTRITIONAL INFORMATION		Serves
Preparation Time 10 minutes	**Per Serving** 155 calories, 5.1g fat (of which 2.9g saturates), 24.6g carbohydrate, 0.2g salt	Vegetarian Gluten free	**8**

Home-made Lemonade

4 unwaxed lemons, sliced

150g (5oz) caster sugar

1 Put the lemons and sugar in a pan with 1.1 litres (2 pints) water. Heat gently to dissolve the sugar, then boil for 2 minutes. Leave to infuse for 30 minutes.

2 Strain the lemonade into a bowl or jug and chill until ready to serve.

Serves 12	EASY		NUTRITIONAL INFORMATION	
	Preparation Time 5 minutes	**Cooking Time** 5 minutes, plus infusing and chilling	**Per Serving** 52 calories, 0.1g fat (of which 0g saturates), 13.6g carbohydrate, 0g salt	Vegetarian Gluten free • Dairy free